# FOREWORD

In the compilation of this book several people have
played an important part. My thanks are due to Miss
Joan Batten, who helped on the research and is responsible for the Appendix; to the official Cliff Richard Fan
Club and the International Cliff Richard Fan Club;
and, of course, to Cliff Richard himself, who is the
primary source of the book's facts (though not its
opinions, unless ascribed to him).

DAVID WINTER

# NEW SINGER, NEW SONG

*The Cliff Richard Story*

by

DAVID WINTER

HODDER AND STOUGHTON

SBN 340 10994 7

*Printed in Great Britain*
*for Hodder and Stoughton Limited,*
*St. Paul's House, Warwick Lane, London, E.C.4,*
*by Richard Clay (The Chaucer Press), Ltd.,*
*Bungay, Suffolk*

# CONTENTS

# ILLUSTRATIONS
Between pages 96–97

First night[2]

Cliff at a Maori concert party[3]

A recording session for TV in Germany[3]

Cliff in thoughtful mood[3]

Sightseeing in Paris[3]

Cliff signing autograph[4]

Cliff relaxing with a cup of tea

Eurovision Song Contest[5]

Cliff at the Billy Graham Crusade[1]

*Key to acknowledgements:*

1 Vincent Hayhurst
2 Napier Russell
3 Dezo Hoffman Ltd.
4 Associated British Pictures
5 Central Press Photos

# INTRODUCTION

In August 1958 a young eighteen-year-old pop singer from Cheshunt, near London, began his career in show business with a four-week engagement at Butlin's Holiday Camp, Clacton. He was supported by his enthusiastic, if technically limited, rock 'n roll group. At the same time their first record, a strident, almost incoherent rock 'n roll number, was released.

The singer's name was Cliff Richard. Shaking his Brylcreemed locks, fixing his wide, dark eyes in a moody glare at the middle distance, waving his arms and sometimes his trunk, and stamping, jerking and rotating his way from stage to stage and town to town, he was soon wildly acclaimed by the teen-agers.

The critics, however, were suitably cynical. They doubted his talent, his resilience, his choice of songs, his voice, his temperament and just about everything else too. 'Rock 'n roll will soon die,' they said. 'Cliff Richard will die with it,' they added. It did; but he did not.

Nine years later his records still regularly reach the top ten in the hit parade. He is still regularly voted 'top British male singer' of the year in the influential annual poll of the *New Musical Express*. He is still one of the highest paid and most eagerly sought after entertainers in Europe. And he also currently holds the Radio Luxembourg award for the entertainer who during the year has done most to enhance the reputation of pop music. The boy from Cheshunt who erupted on to the scene in 1958 as a wild rock 'n roller has become rich and famous.

Riches and fame are not the end of the Cliff Richard story, however, and there lies a further fascination for the biographer.

'The things I had,' he says, 'money, fame, fans—just weren't satisfying me.'

Perhaps the most recent part of Cliff's story—his grappling with a problem that has perplexed many successful men before him : if satisfaction is not at the top of the ladder, where do you look next?—is the most revealing and rewarding of all.

To survive as a top star for nine years in the passing world of pop is a tremendous achievement in itself, and suggests talent and temperament of a high calibre (despite the gloomy prophecies of the critics). But to do it with modesty, self-control and dignity; to abandon one enormously popular style as a rock 'n roller and graduate to maturity as an all-round entertainer; to keep his crown and his head at the same time : this is (to say the least) highly unusual. Modern pop music is dedicated to turning persons into personalities, but all the way up the ladder—and with a normal quota of faults and failings on each rung—Cliff has remained a person, and a very interesting one, too.

The author was teaching at a secondary modern school near Cliff Richard's home area during the period of his dramatic rise to fame. For those of us who were in touch with teen-agers at this time it seemed that Cliff epitomised the whole rock 'n roll era. On stage and on the television screen he seemed to be visualising and vocalising the incoherent voice of a multitude. Youth was flexing its muscles, sensing its new power and influence, testing the extent of its new independence. Cliff—legs astride, voice aggressive and emotional, arms pleading and challenging, body flexed as though against a tide of outraged tradition—became the symbol of the new teen-ager.

And he was new, too. This was the first generation of 'blitz babies'—born in the war, reared while father was away in the Forces—to reach the outskirts of adulthood. They were richer, better educated, more independent than any generation of youngsters had ever been. Theirs was a new world, and it needed a new folk music. Cliff, more than anybody else in his day, seemed to usher in that new world and new music.

Anyone who cares to play one of the top popular records of the immediate post-war years (probably a crooner or a big band) and follow it with a rock 'n roll record or one of the later beat creations of the Beatles or the Rolling Stones will see what a vast difference there is in the outlook of those born before and those born during or after the war. This *is* a new world. For better or worse, its mood and pulse is captured by elemental noise and throbbing beat, not by angelic choirs and smooth saxophones.

Almost all young people today, including many who secretly prefer classical music, pay at least ritual tribute to the current pop musical fashion. (One recollects the hooting scorn of an audience of schoolgirls at one of their number who, in a TV competition, could not name the four Beatles). Pop music, which in its teen-age sector virtually means beat music, is a symbol of the solidarity of youth. The record player is the local altar of this religion, the discotheque its temple, and the top performers its high priests. A whole cultic language, a complete range of publications, special clothes and even a distinctive expression of face are involved in its practice.

It would be quite wrong, however, to imply that only teen-agers now enjoy this sort of music. Those who enjoyed it as teen-agers continue, for the most part, to enjoy it as adults; though in a less hectic, emotionally involved sort of way. After all, the girls who screamed Cliff to the top in 1958 are now, for the most part, sober housewives coping with the family, more concerned with the position of their mini-skirted infants in the fancy dress than of their former idol in the hit parade. Yet many of them—as well as multitudes of those much older—continue to prefer pop to any other sort of music.

But it is the teen-agers, with more spare money for this sort of thing, who are still the mass market for records, and it is with them and their tastes that the commercial manipulators of pop are primarily concerned. The youngsters still set the pace, and establish the latest idol on his insecure throne.

Cliff has somehow managed to keep on his, however, surviving many changing tastes and fashions and several glittering new-comers who have blazed like rockets to the top; and, like rockets, have burnt out and plunged back into obscurity. It seems that his place at the top table is assured—until he feels the moment has come to retire and train to be a teacher.

Beat music, from the primitive rock 'n roll of the fifties to the more sophisticated rhythms of today, has brought enormous pleasure to millions of people. It has involved several thousand of them in the performing of it, in the countless groups that have sprung up in every town and district of the land. It has brought a note of realism and robustness to Tin Pan Alley, in contrast with the lush trivialities of the dance music which preceded it in popular esteem

It has also earned fortunes for song publishers and record manufacturers, for disc jockeys and agents, for writers and performers. This has inevitably brought a sordid and sometimes crooked element into what was, in essence, a spontaneous, genuine movement.

Beat music has also, on the debit side, been the occasion, if not the cause of outbreaks of teen-age violence and rioting and lately has even played a small part, through a few erotic lyrics and some suggestive presentations, in eroding the moral fabric of society.

In other words, as with most aspects of human

experience, there are things to praise and things to blame in beat and other pop music. Except as they arise incidentally to the story, it is not the task of this book to make those sort of judgements.

It would be sad if the era of beat music, and the whole teen-age movement which brought it into being, passed without being chronicled. It is unusual, to say the least, to write a biography of a man still in his twenties; and equally unusual to attempt a portrait of a pop singer *as a person* as well as a performer. Yet what better way is there to capture a little of the flavour of the brave new teen-age world of the late fifties and sixties than through the career and personality of one of its biggest and most representative figures. In passing, we may also discover what qualities there are in Cliff Richard that have made him, not a momentary rocket, but a lasting star in the pop world.

Yet in the last analysis people are interested most of all in people. This book simply would not write itself as the 'history of the pop era', nor as an 'analysis of success'. It wrote itself, for better or worse, as the story of a human being, born Harry Rodger Webb, and growing up to experience more vividly than most of us the depths and heights of ordinary human joys and sorrows, successes and failures. It is not the story of a star—remote, glittering—but the story of the making of a man.

## CHAPTER I

# BUS RIDE TO HODDESDON

HE supposed he would be sick. It was all right for Terry and Norman, sitting in the seat in front laughing about it. But as the bus vibrated through the lower gears away from the stop Harry Webb was already laying plans in his mind to counteract its dire effects on his digestive system.

He looked out of the window. To the right, through the gathering darkness, the roofs of houses and the first of the nurseries. On the left, a few shops and then, quite soon, open fields, before the houses began again at Turnford.

He knew what he had to do: take his mind off it. That was what everybody said. But it was not easy, with the bus shuddering and swaying and waves of nausea flowing across his body and cold sweat on his forehead.

He tried the first gambit. Think about tonight's engagement. The Five Horseshoes at Hoddesdon, play and sing all the evening, beating out pseudo-Presley while the patrons talked and laughed and played darts and sank gallons of mild and bitter in the adjacent bar. Not that he noticed what they did. Once the first few bars were out of his system, and Terry was belting away at his drum-set (*that* put them back a few quid) and the beat was settling into a groove, they could have been at the Palladium for all he knew or cared.

Mind you, they would get paid more at the Palladium. Sometimes at the Five Horseshoes they did quite well—a fiver or so. Sometimes it was just a few shillings. Harry managed a private grin: imagine signing Elvis up on those terms—whatever silver was left in the till when cashing up had followed chucking out.

Not that they worried. They could do with the money, of course—new equipment, Elvis-type outfits and so on, cost plenty of it. But they did not sing for the money. Taking all in all, they hardly earned what they spent on these outings. They sang, with all the exuberance of teen-agers, in an atmosphere thick with cigarette smoke and reeking of liquor. But Harry did not smoke, and he did not drink. There were better things to spend money on, he reckoned.

Harry's stomach reasserted itself. He fervently hoped he would not have to repeat last week's farce. As the bus had stopped to pick up a passenger at Turnford one green-faced young man had jumped off, been violently sick in the gutter and jumped back on again, pale, wobbly and embarrassed. He tried to imagine what Elvis would have done in those circumstances and decided the circumstances would never have arisen. Elvis did not have to go to his engagements on a London Transport Country Green bus. Presumably his chauffeur could always pull off into a roadhouse if the maestro felt a little off-colour.

Harry's experience of travel sickness was a long one. There was, for instance, that journey home from India as a wide-eyed seven-year-old, back in 1947. For the first few days at sea Harry and his mother were so sick it would have been a relief if the boat had sunk. To make matters worse, his father and sister Donella (who had been reckoned until then the family weakling) were almost disgustingly well, enjoying the trip and full of enthusiasm. After they had been at sea three or four days Dad decided his son had been ill long enough. He hauled him out of the cabin, dragged him up on deck and then walked him round and round the ship. Incredibly, within a few hours Harry felt perfectly well and was tucking into his first real meal at sea.

Now *that* was not a helpful thought, he decided, as the bus slowed down in a crescendo of vibration at the junction with the Great Cambridge Road. For one thing, you cannot go for a walk on the roof of a London bus.

Harry could not remember much about India, beyond flying kites, singing in the choir and the 'Home Rule' riots. The kites were wonderful Indian ones, not these pallid imitations they toyed with at the recreation ground. Indian kites are single sail ones with small tail-pieces: the easiest kites in the world to fly and to manoeuvre. The Indians—not only the children, either—stage battles with them, rubbing ground glass into the kite strings and then, from suitable vantage points such as opposing corners of a field, or even adjoining roofs of houses, two kite-flyers will set out to cut each other's string.

Harry could not remember much about the church choir, beyond the red cassock and white surplice and a vague recollection that the church was called St. Thomas's. At any rate, he knew that he went to St. Thomas's church school. He did not go to church nowadays—he had not since he was about fifteen. He used to go with his mother, but life was pretty hectic now, what with all the rehearsing and so on. After all, if you want to get to the top it is all or nothing.

As a family, they used to be quite religious, really. Dad refused to go to church—'not for people like me' —and often used to argue with the vicar when he called; yet it was also Father who used to lead family Bible readings at night-time. The rest of them used to go to church quite regularly, especially when they first moved to the council house in Cheshunt.

He supposed he believed in God—at any rate, he had never decided *not* to—and from time to time he would pray. One day, perhaps—when he had reached the top, or blown up in the attempt—he would like to think this religion business through properly.

Harry drew his knees up and sank even lower in the seat. They were through Wormley now, which meant about another quarter of an hour. He should survive this time.

In a way, he wished he could remember more about the 'Home Rule' riots. After all, if it had not been for them he would presumably still be living in India, and his father would still be working in catering with Kellner's, in Cawnpore, Jaipur, Howrah, Calcutta or some such place.

But he could remember one incident. Out shopping with his mother, they were suddenly surrounded by a crowd of Indians who jostled them. One of them shouted, 'Why don't you go home to your own country, white woman?'

That was exactly what the Webbs decided to do, though not without a trauma or two. Family inquests on the situation balanced the economics—a good job for Dad, a comfortable home, the security of familiarity in a land they had all been born and reared in; against the politics—the growing violence, the uncertainty about the future and the doubts about whether British people would be welcome in India when Home Rule finally arrived. The unwelcome conclusion was that the time had come to leave India.

Mum, he recalled, favoured the advice gratuitously offered by the vocal gentleman in the shop: she was all for going 'home', which was a country—Britain— that none of them had ever seen.

The only alternative—the one his father favoured at first—was Australia. A friend of the family was going there and had even offered to pay their fare.

England won. Harry looked out of the window at the traffic stream edging its way sulphurously towards the traffic lights at Broxbourne, a mile away, and wondered why.

The Webb family had wondered why, too; and his mother still often regretted it. There was a time, just after they arrived in England, when she cried every day for sheer frustration and dislike of the place! It was not surprising, after all. In India they had lived in comparative luxury. After selling up, and making that strange voyage 'home', they arrived on English soil with just five pounds in their pockets. They literally did not know where the next meal was coming from.

It was Tilbury—not exactly Britain's top beauty spot—that gave them their first real taste of the homeland, but it was the green fields and trees of the countryside through which they travelled on their way to his grandmother's place in Carshalton that first struck them about England.

Grandma nobly received the Webb family into her home, and for eighteen months they lived in Carshalton. Harry vividly remembered his first taste of English school-life—at Stanley Park Road Primary School, Carshalton.

They say your schooldays are the happiest time of your life. Despite his internal disturbances, Harry managed a wry grin into the window at the thought of it. Later on, he quite enjoyed school, but those first few months in primary school would be remembered to his dying day.

The great sin among children is to be different—to speak or act or look differently. Now that there were more coloured people about it did not seem so strange, but then anybody with a dark skin or an unfamiliar accent was a 'wog'. The children in Carshalton had the pink pallor of suburbia. Harry's skin was dark brown from the hot sun of India. The others talked the bloodless dialect of outer London. Harry spoke with the sing-song dialect of the English Indians—not unlike a sort of muted Welsh accent.

Anyway, he was marked out as 'different'. With all the fierceness of remembered injustices Harry recalled the baiting and jeering.

'Where yer from, mate?'

'India.'

'Cor, did yer live in a wigwam then?'

Fruitlessly he would try to explain the difference between India and America, and between English people living in India and Red Indians living in the Wild West. It was of no avail.

'Where's yer head-dress, then?'

'Red Indian Harry!'

'Nigger, nigger!'

The shouts echoed across the years. They had made playtime a small boy's hell. They followed him home each night. And inevitably they had led to quarrels and fights—endless fights, with all the tormented malice of little boys in them.

But the worst moment—nine years later it was still vivid—was when one of the teachers joined in, and made a joke in class about Harry Webb and his wigwam.

At least it had taught him one thing—the sheer ugliness of racial prejudice. If he became famous . . .

he corrected himself, *when* he became famous . . . he would remember that. To judge a person by the colour of his skin or hair was ignorant, and its results were bitter and cruel. There are some lessons only experience can teach really well, and this was one Harry Webb had assimilated the hard way.

The teasing died out eventually, possibly because Harry lost his tropical tan and adopted the local patois. His mother had told him that within a year of returning to England he was sporting a really dreadful sub-Cockney accent. He had not got a *bad* accent now, he thought. The mixture of his childhood speech and the various parts of the London area in which they had since lived had produced a fairly neutral 'South-East England' sort of accent which was pretty standard among his friends and accomplices.

They had stayed at Carshalton eighteen months, when they finally decided they could not impose on Grandma any longer. Not only had she housed them but, during a period when Harry's father had found it very difficult to get and hold a job, she had also helped out with small luxuries—his cigarettes, for instance—which they could never have afforded. For six or seven months of that period Dad was completely unemployed. All his experience in India was useless in the England of 1948. Catering in Calcutta was a vastly different business from catering in Carshalton, especially in those post-war austerity years of ration books, 'points' and so on.

The Webbs moved to Waltham Cross, on the

north-eastern suburbs of London in the Lea Valley, to live with an aunt who had suggested they might have a chance of finding better accommodation in that district. Harry's father, too, had been offered a steady job at Ferguson's radio and television factory at Enfield, just a mile or two away, so the move had seemed a logical one.

It seemed strange to Harry, looking back, that just as he was getting on terms with his school-mates, and beginning to master the intricacies of arithmetic with British money, he should be whisked across London to another environment, another 'temporary' home and another school.

The home was hardly an improvement, for the five of them lived in one room . . . and fairly soon a sixth joined them, in the person of baby Joan. Then it really *was* chaotic! They had put their names down for a council house, but the consensus of opinion in the butcher's queue was that you had to have lived in the district for ten years to have a ghost of a chance. Alternatively, it was suggested, one could pester the housing officer day in and day out until he allocated a house in sheer self-defence.

Harry's mother was not prepared to do the latter, and the former course would appear to qualify the Webbs for a house in the late nineteen-fifties. As the children fell over each other, and Mum and Dad fell over the children, this seemed a dismal prospect.

As the bus finally inched over the Broxbourne traffic lights, and Harry breathed an audible sigh of

relief that they were on their way again, he also recalled that it was at Broxbourne, in a small factory,
that his mother got a job as soon as she sensibly could
after Joan was born.

With Dad out at work all day until seven-thirty in
the evening, and Mum leaving for work soon after
four p.m., to put in a regular evening shift at the
factory, that left Harry as senior officer commanding
for three hours or so each day. When he got home
from school he would get supper for the two smallest
girls and generally cope with them until Dad got
home.

This sort of Box-and-Cox situation, in which
mother and father barely saw each other except on
Sundays, could have led to family tensions. In fact,
Harry thought, it had knit them together.

They had always been a 'close' family. As the eldest
child, Harry had always shared in family discussions
and problems, and during this difficult period at
Waltham Cross the bond between father, mother and
their ten-year-old son grew very strong. Harry was
pleased that they trusted him, and a common foe—
despair—united them.

They were still close. Sometimes, even now, he got
ribbed about the way he constantly referred to 'my
Mum' and 'my Dad', but if his friends had been
through what the Webbs had been through they
would understand.

Mum had cycled to work at Broxbourne, about five
miles, and sometimes he had cycled to meet her half-

way on her way home late at night: but that was later, he remembered, when he was at secondary school— and after they had moved into a house.

That had seemed almost a miracle at the time. A council housing officer had called one day, apparently as a result of a neighbour reporting the appalling conditions in which the Webbs were living. After a swift analysis of their situation and a quick look at the room they were living in he assured them they would have a council house 'within two months'. He kept his word, too, so that very soon the Webbs were able to move into the first home of their own in England, on a council estate in Cheshunt. It was red-brick, two down and three up, with a very small garden. But for the Webbs it was little short of paradise on earth.

Paradise turned sour for a while not long after, however. It was not one of Harry's favourite memories. Those were the days of the eleven-plus— the examination taken by all primary school children when they reached the age of eleven, on the basis of which they were allocated to grammar, technical or secondary modern schools. Harry had been at Kings Road School, Waltham Cross, since they moved from Carshalton, and a few months before the eleven-plus he had been awarded a prize for being the school's top boy in class work. Yet when the examination results were published he discovered to his abject horror that he had failed to win a grammar-school place.

He was completely shattered; his confidence and bounce failed him, for once. He was ashamed, too, and felt he had let his parents down. He had always been comparatively weaker under examination conditions, possibly because he was very nervous.

Not only that, but when he had arrived at his new school—Cheshunt Secondary Modern—he was equally shattered to find he was not in the top 'stream', but in what was called 'Upper B'. However, he consoled himself, half-way through the first term he had been transferred to the A-stream.

Cheshunt was a good school, and he had enjoyed that part of his school career. Indeed, he had been terrified at the thought of leaving, as he had no inclination to do anything but be a pop-singer, and how could you tell the careers master and juvenile employment exchange *that*? He had enjoyed English and maths and liked most of his teachers, but, looking back, the best thing about that school was the friends he made and the opportunities for singing.

The other really enjoyable thing about school was the sport. Harry was good at most sports, and quite outstanding at soccer—he had even played for the county, Hertfordshire schoolboys. He supposed that if he had not got this compulsive urge to be a singer he might have had an equally compulsive urge to be a professional footballer.

He could not remember exactly when this singing business began, nor how. His mother said he sang melodiously in the bath from an early age. For himself, the earliest recollections of a real interest in the subject were linked with the name of Elvis Presley, and miming his big hits in front of the family gramophone.

He had sung as a child at school, of course, and, going far back, in the church choir in India. He could remember his voice breaking, exactly half-way through a rather dreary hymn in assembly at school when he was thirteen: suddenly the insecure falsetto of puberty evaded him, and the next note emerged as a slightly desperate croak.

But the croak gave way to what seemed to be quite a melodious male voice. It was not only Harry who thought so. His mother did—but then, she would. But Mrs. Norris thought so too: and that was different.

Mrs. Norris was his English teacher. Possibly because he was quite good at English—he got his G.C.E. in that subject, he reminded himself—she took quite an interest in him. He still looked her up from time to time.

When he was about fourteen the school dramatic society produced *Wind in the Willows*. Someone had talked him into joining the society, and he was given the part of Ratty. This called for him to sing a couple of simple songs, and it was after the performance that Mrs. Norris came up to him and said that he had a nice voice and 'had he thought of taking up singing?'

Had he *thought* of it? Yes, he had, endlessly. From about the time he went to secondary school he had been passionately interested in pop music—especially the new Elvis beat style. This was the beginning of the new sound in pop, the strident electric music and

crashing throb of rock 'n roll. He remembered hearing
different artists on the radio and saying—boastfully,
he supposed, but absolutely sincerely—'I could do
that.' Once he had looked at a picture of Elvis receiving some show-business award and had remarked
to his friends, 'I'll do that one day.' They thought it
was a good joke.

It did not look quite such a good one on an evening
like this. There must be literally hundreds of beat
groups like theirs around the London area alone. Who
was going to notice them on their exotic tours of the
north London suburbs? But there was nothing else,
no other ambition.

When, he asked himself, had this utter determination been born? To want to be a big star was one
thing—for all he knew every other boy in the school
shared that as a hope. But he had long realised that
not many shared his conviction that it could actually
happen, and to him. It was in obedience to that conviction that he now sat on a seat by the window of a
No. 310 bus and felt very, very sick, on his way to a
two-hour sweat session, in a not very notable tavern.
Ambition takes some odd routes to the top.

One significant step in the growth of the ambition
was the day he went to see a stage show by Bill Haley
and the Comets, just about the first beat group, in the
full sense of the word, to hit the British scene. The
excitement Haley and his men caused among the teen-
agers—the feeling of being in on the birth of something really new and exciting—was tremendous. Then

came the news that Bill Haley and his Comets were to do a show at Edmonton—just a couple of miles away.

Harry and a few of his friends—all prefects at Cheshunt—decided that, come what may, this was a show they were not going to miss. Rock 'n roll was still quite new, and the papers were full of stories about screaming teen-agers and roaring, jigging, jubilant audiences. Harry and his friends decided to give school a miss for the morning and queue for tickets. They got up very early, and arrived at the theatre before six a.m.—and yet there was already a queue, largely of fans who had been there all night. For some reason the box office did not open at the advertised time—eleven—and they did not get their tickets until half-past, but they finally emerged triumphant, clutching five-shilling tickets which they would not have sold for ten times that amount.

By the time they got back to Harry's for an alfresco lunch they had decided there was no point in going back to school for the remainder of the afternoon. In any case, the show was tonight and painful irrelevances like giving an account of their absence could not be allowed to mar its anticipation. They could talk and think of nothing else.

Harry would never forget that night. They caught the bus to Edmonton and joined hundreds of other teen-agers waiting for the doors to open. Even then the atmosphere was heady, the whole crowd of them drunk with expectancy, toe-tapping, boisterous: yet united in anticipation and impatience.

It was a bit less united when the doors opened, and all the five bobs stormed the gallery staircase to get the best seats. Then came the waiting, and the tension and longing building up again, until the curtains swung back, the spotlights reflected on chrome and silverplate, and the first glorious, strident, earthy beat of the Comets swept across the audience. The effect was electric. The entire theatre seemed to erupt in a thunderclap of sound—the beat of the bass and rhythm guitars, the percussion, the wailing saxophones, only just audible above the flood-tide of yelling, exulting youngsters. It was as though all the pent-up colour and fervour and passion of a thousand grey young suburban lives were released in a dynamic moment of truth. This was their music, and their moment.

It was then, in that single second, that Harry knew exactly what he wanted to do more than anything in the world. An ambition, a vague, half-formed hope, became an irresistible conviction. To be the hub and centre of that ecstatic moment of life—there was an ambition worth living and working for.

Most of the others in his form were keen on pop music, favouring Dickie Valentine or Elvis Presley or Bill Haley or another of the idols of the day. Many of them talked show business, record charts and even the technicalities of skiffle and rock 'n roll. But Harry guessed that few of them were dedicating themselves, as he was, not to being a fan, but a performer.

He could still see his mother's face when she burst

into the front room and found him singing a duet with Elvis Presley—the American, of course, was on disc, but it was the only way Harry could make use of Elvis's backing. He began to cultivate the Elvis hairstyle, sideburns and all, and worked hard at the Presley 'look'—the moody, smouldering expression. He also imitated the Presley mannerisms, and on one or two occasions when he managed to get photographed in a typical pose of the maestro he really felt it was worth while. 'You look just like Elvis'—no higher compliment could he conceive.

His mother backed his ambitions to the hilt. She claimed, with some justification, that she had seen a singing career for him even before he had. She entered him for a talent competition. He still squirmed slightly at the memory of it. Mother was sure he would win, Harry thought he might do quite well, and they were both proved wrong.

What discourages the uncommitted merely spurs the dedicated. Harry just tried harder. Despite Dad's wise warning—'Don't pin too much faith in it, Harry, you might be terribly disappointed'—the ambition grew and grew, until it dominated all his thinking about the future. Indeed, he was terrified at the thought of leaving school, because he refused to contemplate any job other than singing and yet knew that an office or the bank or a factory almost certainly lay before him. Despite this, his school work began to suffer as it became obvious his interests lay elsewhere. The Bill Haley incident was only one example of this.

The next morning the delinquents had to parade before the Head. He dressed them down at length (which they had expected) and then took away their prefects' badges (which they had not). Harry recalled that he had dared to protest.

'I don't think that's fair,' he had objected. 'I bet if we'd been to the Bolshoi Ballet you'd have given us a pat on the back.'

But protests were of no avail. Beat or Bolshoi, they had 'set a bad example', and the nakedness of their blazer lapels told its own embarrassing story to the whole school.

Mrs. Norris, too, had volunteered a few words of mild rebuke. She shook her head sadly when he returned to the classroom minus his prefect's badge.

'In ten years' time, Harry,' she had told him, 'I'll bet you won't even remember the name of Bill Haley.'

Knowing how far he could go with her, he had had the cheek to bet her a box of chocolates that he would. He reckoned he would collect it, too—in 1966!

Harry grinned into the bus window. His stomach was behaving itself quite well, really. After all, the bus was grinding up the hill towards Hoddesdon High Street and so far he had not actually felt too bad ... with only about half a mile to go. As usual, Terry, Norman and Ian were laughing and larking about. They were good friends and shared his ambitious determination to reach the top. He had had to look for a long time to find a group who did.

The first group he had belonged to had been called

the Quintones. He still winced at the name. Three girls and two boys (hence the title) from school, they became quite popular at school concerts and other local events—unaccompanied, and with Harry contributing the occasional solo. His favourite of their numbers, he recalled, was (not surprisingly) 'Heartbreak Hotel', one of Elvis's hits. They even put themselves up for a television talent competition, *Opportunity Knocks*, run by Hughie Green. (Come to think of it, they had never heard from him.) He still saw several of the Quintones around—one of the girls was starting training as a nurse soon.

But that was strictly small-time. The second group he was in was a bit more serious. It was called the Dick Teague Skiffle Group. Skiffle was a style of music he all but despised. He recalled how he had come to join the group. It was on a bus in Cheshunt. He had met Terry Smart's girl friend—Terry was a school friend—and she had told him that Terry was playing the drums in a local skiffle group and he had said that he would very much like Harry to join him.

The idea was intriguing. Harry knew Terry as a pretty wild drummer who favoured the rock. He could not really see him being at home in a skiffle group, complete with tea-chest bass, washboard and country rhythm. Neither could he see himself—the Enfield Elvis—in that setting.

It was not that he actively disliked skiffle, but it never raised his pulse rate like rock. Harry's singing was distinctly spontaneous in style, and there was nothing in skiffle to put fire and invention into what was otherwise just a pleasant tenor register voice. But if Terry thought it worthwhile being in a skiffle group, then he could not dismiss the idea.

After all, for a long time Harry had been looking for a way to get his foot at least on the bottom rung of the show-business ladder, and the Dick Teague Skiffle Group represented just about that. Terry, too, was ambitious, and he had thought it worthwhile to join the group. If he could play the drums and keep one eye on the second rung, then Harry could sing the solos and keep his eye on the same spot. Who knows, with two members forming a sort of rock 'n roll fifth column, the Dick Teague Skiffle Group might advance—possibly without knowing it—into something rather more exhilarating.

There was another factor. Singing at school concerts, miming to other people's records (or singing duets with the record player) was one thing, but nobody got spotted that way. If he were to sing regularly with an established group, however humble, then at least this was the real thing, and he could judge himself, and others could judge him, by professional standards.

The Dick Teague Skiffle Group won, and its new soloist, Harry Webb, began to take the rostrum at weddings, children's parties, twenty-first birthdays, badminton club suppers and the like—strictly within two miles of Cheshunt, of course. This was not exactly big time, but it *was* that bottom rung, and at sixteen he did not expect to walk into the West End.

Funnily enough, it was because of joining the skiffle group that Harry had learned to play the guitar. He had had to do an audition—his first ever—and was highly delighted to be told by Dick Teague that he would 'do fine'. Home he went to break the good news to his parents (the contempt for skiffle forgotten in the sweet moment of success) and only came down to earth when Terry explained that he would have to play the guitar as well. This presented two major difficulties. In the first place, Harry did not possess a guitar. In the second place, if he had, he would not have been able to play it.

Dad and Terry came to his aid. Terry produced a guitar—an old one that cost five guineas several years before. Dad organised practice sessions, hour after hour, in the living room. Within a few days Harry had mastered three primary chords. Within three weeks he could manage three different keys. Armed with this rather limited expertise, Cheshunt and District's latest and most optimistic skiffle soloist took his appointed place with the Dick Teague Skiffle Group. He was a *singer* at last.

## CHAPTER II

## THE FIVE HORSESHOES

'WAKE up, Harry. We're getting off!'

Harry peered up over his collar. A glance out of the window confirmed that they were telling the truth.

'Half a mo',' he mumbled, rising inelegantly to his feet. 'Don't forget the amplifier.'

Down the stairs they stumbled, and out into the clear evening air. Already Harry was feeling better. He had managed the journey, he had not been sick, an evening's beat lay ahead. His spirits picked up visibly.

'Here, let me take that one—no, it's all right, I feel fine now.'

That was one thing about skiffle—the gear was simple. But with beat you had to carry half an electronics factory around with you. Down the road from the Clock Tower and into the pub they staggered, laughing a little too noisily, and began setting up the equipment. Already there was quite a good crowd there, including some younger people who seemed to come especially when they were there. 'Our fans,' they called them.

It was not an ideal place to perform, by any means. Harry hated cigarettes—he could remember a time

when even to pass an ash-tray made him feel sick—
and the air always filled with an acrid smoke haze by
mid-evening. The smell of stale beer was not much
better. But on the other hand, the customers seemed
to like their music, and appreciation is nine-tenths of
the beat battle. And it was an engagement—a paid
engagement—a rung (number two? number three?)
on the ladder they were all intent on climbing to the
top.

After the usual alarms and excursions over the
amplifier, and the inevitable juggling with plugs and
sockets, they were off. As the first electronic sound
wave broke from the guitars and the drum began its
insistent, assertive spasm, Harry stepped up to the
microphone. This was going to be a good night. He
felt it. He was nervous, but that was a good sign . . . a
little, tight cough, a clearing of the throat, the catching
of the rhythm and then the first clear, boyish bars;
until, like a surf rider, swept along on the fast flowing
tide, he rode exultantly through the lyric.

This, for Harry, was the magic of beat music, being
lost in an exciting world of colour and sound, and yet
not lost and frightened like a small child, but lost and
liberated like an escaped prisoner.

The customers began to catch his mood, and to
share the sheer youthful joy of it. The songs were
second-hand, mostly Presley's; but the experience was
mint-new. The singer's exhilaration was infectious.
On cold analysis he was raw, amateur, gauche. But in
the bright, warm room, with the air shivering with

sound, cold analysis would have been impossible. In the face of something as elemental as sound itself, as artless and ingenuous as breathing, it was hard to remain aloof.

As the number ended, and the applause bounced back like a recoil, Harry glanced at his colleagues. The perspiration glinted on their foreheads, but the same earthy joy shone in their eyes as in his. Never more than at that moment had he felt them to be so much a team.

Terry Smart was the drummer, of course, and one of his oldest friends. They had kept together since the Dick Teague Skiffle Group days, which was just after Harry and Terry left school. Neither of them was really sold on skiffle, and after the initial novelty of performing in public had worn off, they both began to get rather disenchanted with its bloodless cadences. Harry's singing began to revert to his erstwhile Presley style, which, with skiffle backing, was like singing the Hallelujah Chorus to a minuet. The group, not unreasonably, objected. After a spirited discussion on the relative merits of the different styles, the soloist and the drummer parted company with the rest of the group. There were few regrets on either side.

By now Terry and he had set their minds on forming their own group, and it would not be one of these tea-chest and washboard outfits. His mother and father had not objected—'Well, why not?' they had replied when he had put to them his show-business ambitions—and it fitted in with the slowly maturing plans he had laid for his ascent of the ladder. They enrolled another old school friend, Norman Mitham, as rhythm guitarist, and got down to serious practice.

Their style was strictly rock 'n roll, with the maximum output of decibels at every opportunity. Their repertoire was the top pops of the day—and it still was, really.

Life began to slip into its present routine. He would get up quite early to leave for work at Ferguson's with his father. After work it would be a quick meal and a performance somewhere—club, dance or pub—when they could get a booking; or else a slightly less abbreviated supper and a full evening's practice.

*That* led to some complications, too. When their instruments were plugged in and switched on, and they were really moving it, the sound-proofing qualities of the six-inch brick walls of a terraced council house were shown to be strictly limited. The little house did its own rocking, and the whole road would know that 'young Harry Webb and his friends were playing their guitars.'

Not surprisingly, somebody complained, and the result from a call from a Town Hall official who wanted to find out if it were true that a beat spectacular was rocking the estate three nights out of four. He found it was; but he also found three earnestly dedicated young men, all equally convinced that, given plenty of opportunities to practise, they could put Britain on the pop-music map.

Their story must have been a good one. The official

relented, and fixed a very satisfactory compromise. Practice was permitted, with the doors and windows closed, but it must end at ten o'clock. The neighbours were relieved, the lads were delighted and the remainder of the Webb family swallowed hard and managed to live through it. Incredibly, neither Mum nor Dad ever complained, although, with windows shut and sealed and plenty of energy being burnt up, on some nights the house was incredibly hot, and always it was ringing with sound.

Harry glanced at Norman, who was tuning up for the next number. Norman was not a very good guitarist, but he was a hard worker, loyal and patient, and he made the right sort of noises come out of his instrument at more or less the right moments. If ever they got their big break, Norman's limitations might be embarrassing. But at the moment nobody really worried.

A nod from Norman that all was well, a really exciting roll on the drums from Terry and they were off again. Through the haze and the sweat he could see the faces of the listeners, and sensed the power over them that rhythm gave the players.

It reminded him of one of the most satisfactory evenings of his life. It was not all that long ago—six or seven months, perhaps. They had been booked to play at a dance jointly with another group, each playing for a while and then handing over to the others.

Nobody could remember afterwards how it began, but, egged on by some of the customers, the two groups gradually got drawn into a real battle of beat, with each trying to outdo the other. This went on for several hours, to the huge delight of the onlookers. The noise was deafening, the atmosphere electric, as guitars wailed louder and louder and solo voice tried to cap solo voice. Since then they had often played better, but never, he guessed, had they played longer or louder! He had lost his voice by the time he got home.

It was about then that they got a chance to play at the 21's espresso bar down in Soho. Of course, hundreds of groups had played there, and there was nothing very special about getting a chance to perform. But there was a certain aura about the place and the very name: had not Tommy Steele himself become a star almost overnight through singing at the 21's?

They often talked, and he often dreamed, of the way they would be discovered. Outwardly, they never admitted to any doubts that it would happen. Inwardly Harry, at least, sometimes despaired. The West End, star billing, records, shows: it all seemed a million miles from Cheshunt, Wormley and Hoddesdon, and badminton-club dinners and twenty-first birthday parties. They were young—Harry was barely seventeen—but the rock 'n roll world was a young one, too. They began to feel that if they did not break into the London picture soon they would never get beyond the Cheshunt milk-round.

So they pinned a great deal—too much—on this

21's opportunity. Harry had felt desperately sick all the way to London on the Green Line bus, but he had thought they had played well enough. They had played all the big Elvis hits, in the Elvis manner, and the audience seemed to have enjoyed it.

They hung around afterwards, waiting for some alert talent scout to snap them up. But the only person who approached them was Ian—Ian Samwell. Harry glanced at him now, fingering the leading theme of the number, gently rocking on his heels.

Ian had been in the R.A.F. then, and he had come up to them after the show to tell them that they needed a lead guitarist (they knew that) and that he was the man (which they could not have known). He was due out of the Air Force fairly soon, and would be delighted to join their group.

They auditioned him on the spot. Probably by top standards he was below average, but to them he had sounded like Segovia. Trying not to look too pleased, they had signed him on.

Now they really had expected stardom, but in fact it was back to the Cheshunt round again. About that time they had acquired their present name as a group. The Drifters—it was mainly Terry's idea, though the dictionary had helped them to improve on their first popular suggestion, the Planets. Terry lived at Flamstead End, Norman and Harry lived on the same council estate, and Ian was at Hendon R.A.F. station; and their sphere of operation was strictly local. They did local shows and hoped and waited. It was the *wait-*

*ing* part that was so difficult.

They had been to this pub a couple of times before. Tonight they were really rocking it, though—there were fewer than usual standing at the bar, and a bigger crowd listening. A sudden, spontaneous, perhaps accidental, collusion of chords caught him enraptured, and one of those fleeting moments of exhilaration submerged words and thoughts.

They played that evening for just under three hours, and would cheerfully have done it for nothing. The impatience at the failure to break into the big time only made itself felt when they were at work, or sitting around talking. When they were playing—at least, when they were *performing*—the venue and setting, and ambition itself, hardly mattered. A pub in a country town seems as unlikely a place as any to turn a major corner in life, or climb a significant rung on the ladder of success; and they were not playing here for talent scouts, nor even for the silver in the till. Yet it was there—such are the tricks of fate—that it all began to happen, and on that very night.

The music room at the Five Horseshoes was an annexe to the right of the main building. It was one of the few pubs in the area at that time to provide entertainment for the clients—there was a billiards room, too, at the other end—and so it drew a clientele on beat nights that was rather different from the usual pub one. The music room was not large—almost square, accommodating a hundred or so, sitting and standing—and it got very warm in the course of an evening. By the time Harry and the boys finished their stint, the crowd was usually beginning to thin, and the landlord's voice would echo through from the bar, 'Last drinks, gentlemen.' Mopping their brows, The Drifters would begin dismantling and packing up their equipment.

On this particular night, as they were doing it, a young man of about their own age, or perhaps a year or two older, pushed his way through to them.

'That's great stuff, boys,' he said. 'Really great. What are you doing about it?'

Harry unbent himself from over the amplifier plugs. Compliments were not two a penny for the group, especially from apparently rational and sober young males.

'Thanks,' he replied. 'Glad you like it.'

'But what are you doing about it?' the stranger asked again.

'Nothing,' said Ian, pausing with a roll of lead in his hands, 'We don't know what to do about it. Any ideas?'

'Yes,' came the reply, 'Let me be your manager.'

'You must be joking!' said Harry, but the young man looked deadly serious. He assured them that it was all on the level, and set about persuading them of two crucial things: firstly, that they were potentially really great; and secondly, that what they needed was a manager who would get them off the Cheshunt circuit and into London, permanently.

His name, they discovered, was Johnny Foster.

They also found out that he was a determined, persuasive person. As they found that his eloquence convinced them, perhaps (they began to reason) it would convince London managers and agents. It was certainly worth a try, and it would cost them nothing. By the time they got on to the 310 bus that night, The Drifters had a manager. But more than that, by some strange trick of hallucination, they had *hope*—real, invincible hope—that things had changed for the better, that the bright lights and the big time now beckoned them as never before.

## CHAPTER III

## GREEN LINE TO LONDON

JOHNNY FOSTER was as good as his word. He and Ian Samwell spent all their spare time visiting agents and trying to talk managers into booking this sensational new group from the groovy Lea Valley. It was hard work, and competition was intense, but by sheer persistence (a quality with which Mr. Foster was well endowed) they were convinced anything was possible.

Actually, the first engagement they had achieved required no skill or eloquence—just the obtaining of an entry form. It was to take part in an amateur talent show at the Trocadero Theatre, Elephant and Castle, in south London.

The group were excited and a little tense about this. For one thing, for all their confidence, they had no real evidence to support their faith in themselves, beyond Johnny Foster's enthusiasm and the unjudging adulation of a small clique of young girls from their own home area. How good were they, compared with all the other hundreds of rock 'n roll and beat groups springing up in those opening years of the big pop music boom? Now they would know, as they took their place in competition with others who had the same ambitions and the same faith in themselves. They began to appreciate the deep truth of the saying 'Where ignorance is bliss . . .'

They had an awful journey from Cheshunt to the Elephant and Castle on the bus and tube, dragging their equipment with them. The sooner they got a nice fat contract and enough in the bank to pay for a van or estate car, the happier they would be. They arrived at the theatre to find it swarming with eager, confident young men, many of them with shining chromium-plated apparatus which had not had to survive manhandling two-thirds of the way across London by public transport.

Johnny Foster's patter kept their spirits up in the face of all this. It was *talent* that counted, he reminded them, not flashy gear. His advice was well intended, and true as far as it went; but it sounded a little thin in the face of the final tragedy—the awful moment of truth, just before they were due on stage, when they plugged in and switched on, and nothing happened at all.

They fiddled with connections, tightened up screws and tried again. Still the amplifier was mute. They tapped it, pummelled it, kicked it and swore at it. Still not one wailing note would it emit. Biting back the tears, they went to the organiser and withdrew from the contest.

Silent with rage and bitter disappointment, they stowed it all away again and crept out of the theatre. As they left, the jaunty strains echoing through the dressing-room corridors did nothing to soothe their wounds.

Harry was not sick as he sat silent and hunched by the window on the top deck of the bus as it ground and trembled its way out through the northern suburbs to Cheshunt that night. He was not sick, but for the first time since childhood he wept, quietly and bitterly. They had failed. They had been humiliated. It was the end of the world. Because they were hard-up, working-class boys, without the money for new equipment, they were being left behind in the race to the top. Self-pity, mortification, jealousy and desperate disappointment flooded his heart. This was the bottom of everything, the lowest ebb.

In fact, that was the plain truth, though neither Harry nor his friends knew it. This *was* the lowest ebb: the last moment of failure; there were no more depths to plumb. From now on it was to be a golden way to glory.

The Drifters' spirits made a typically youthful recovery. The failure, they reasoned, was not in them, but in that shoddy equipment. As they overhauled it and traced the fault, they vowed that their first indulgence when they finally made it would be to get themselves a completely new set of amplifying equipment. Their spirits were also considerably helped by the news from Johnny and Ian that they had obtained a return booking for the 21's. Perhaps *this* time they would be spotted . . .

However, recent events had put a healthy caution

into their optimism, and they were all the more delighted when, at the end of their performance, a real live manager approached them. Would they, he enquired casually, be interested in appearing at a ballroom in Derby? They would, they indicated, a quick check on barely suppressed grins of delight revealing that this agreement was unanimous. They also agreed the terms—indeed, they hardly noticed them, and only found later that the fee just about covered their return rail fares.

'O.K.,' said the manager, whose name was Harry Greatrix, 'That's all fixed. Now, how do I bill you?'

'The Drifters,' Harry answered.

'Yes, kid, I know. But you're singer. How do I bill you?'

'Harry Webb.'

'Harry Webb and the Drifters?' He pondered it a moment without enthusiasm. 'Doesn't sound much good to me.'

Now they came to think about it, it did not sound all that good to them, either. They retired to an adjacent pub—The Swiss—to think this one over.

It was the Harry Webb part that was the trouble. Harry was proud of his family name, though he was not all that 'wild about Harry'. Various suggestions were made to improve on it.

Harry had always liked the name Richard, and preliminary skirmishes centred around finding a surname to go with it (once Richard Webb had been firmly rejected). Suddenly one of them went off on a different track altogether.

'How about Russ Clifford?'

'Not Russ,' Harry objected, 'It's too soft spoken. Why not Cliff Russard?'

Johnny Foster jumped in, tied the two different tracks together, and said, 'Why not Cliff Richard?'

'Richards,' someone objected.

'No, I mean Richard, without the "s". It's just the name we're looking for. Everybody will call him Cliff Richards and then we can correct them—that way they'll never forget his name.'

The argument was a compelling one, the name sounded right, and subsequent history showed just how effective the omission of the 's' was to be from a publicity point of view.

So it was that Cliff Richard and the Drifters made their first public appearance at a ballroom in Derby, as pleased with themselves as if it had been the Palladium, and as elated and confident now as they were depressed and dejected a few weeks before.

The change of name was easy for the group, but difficult for Harry's family. Mother took to it fairly quickly, and Donna was one of his best supporters in the change-over. When asked by another member of the family, 'Where's Harry?' her simple counter was, 'Who's Harry?' For his father it was complicated by the fact that his son was Cliff at home but Harry at work in the factory, but he struggled manfully to adjust himself on the way back home in the evening. For himself, Cliff (as we must now call him) was well pleased. From the moment Johnny Foster first suggested the name he knew it suited him better than Harry had ever done.

Ian and Johnny continued to search for openings. Emboldened by their first 'away' fixture at Derby, where the youngsters had really seemed to like their act, they decided to try again in London. As it happened, they turned their attention to the Gaumont cinema, Shepherd's Bush.

Ian had seen a poster advertising a talent competition. With smarting memories of the Trocadero, he and Johnny had no intention of entering for the competition. Instead, with staggering confidence—or cheek—they cornered the manager in his office and explained that they would not (of course) want to enter a talent competition, but they could be talked into making a personal appearance at the end, just to give the occasion a touch of the big time.

Presumably thinking that any young men as confident as this *must* be good, the manager agreed to their appearing as the 'head of the bill', to play at the end of the competition. There would be no fee, but he would pay their fares. Unable to decline so generous an offer, they allowed themselves to be persuaded into accepting it, and dashed off to Cheshunt to break the tremendous news to the rest of the group.

It was a fair-to-good talent competition. At least all the other acts—looking enviously at the Drifters, standing aside from the rat-race with Olympian detachment—helped to warm up the audience, which seemed to consist very largely of young teen-age girls. By the time Cliff Richard and the Drifters were announced the stage was set for a wild finale.

As they burst into their first number the fans started screaming, and, by the noise, most of them did not stop all through the performance. The boys were really inspired, the insistent, primitive beat of rock 'n roll flooded the huge cinema, and Cliff gave a passable imitation of Elvis, going down on his knees, doing a few steps, throwing his head back and ploughing a lonely, youthful furrow of incoherent sound about four tenor tones above the backing.

As the rhythm built up, so did the excitement. Girls began jumping on their seats, young fellows took to the aisles to sway and dance in time to the beat, and a few got so excited they began damaging the fittings. It was tremendous—'ridiculous', as Cliff now puts it—and very, very noisy. As they stood on the stage surveying the devastating effect of their performance it at last dawned on the Drifters that the top of the rock 'n roll business was not beyond their reach. It was that Saturday morning in the Shepherd's Bush Gaumont that concreted in Cliff's mind, too, the realisation that his hopes and ambitions might have a solid basis.

When they came to try to leave the theatre, they found the stage door besieged by girls. Other teenagers were running wild up and down the street outside. It was all quite unbelievable. They had played the same items dozens of times before, but never with anything like this effect. The patrons of the Five

Horseshoes were not in the habit of dismantling the premises in response to rock 'n roll!

They asked the manager if they could come again and do a show, possibly at the Saturday morning junior teen-agers' club. He counted the takings, assessed the damage, and agreed.

A plan was formulating itself in their minds. If they could persuade an agent to attend their next performance at the Gaumont, and if it produced the same effect on the customers, surely he *must* be impressed? Ian and Johnny dedicated all their considerable powers of persuasion to the task of getting such a man to promise to attend. They succeeded.

The man they persuaded to attend was George Gangou. He was quite a well-known agent, though he was not known for his interest in rock 'n roll: cabaret and even classics had been more in his line of country.

However, he duly turned up at the Gaumont a couple of weeks later and sat in adult isolation as a thousand or so youngsters again erupted at the performance of Cliff and the Drifters. The performers did not feel that it was one of their best efforts, but with the general din created by girlish screams, pounding feet, the noise of seats being banged up and down and the like, the standard of performance was less important than its unquestionable impact on the paying customers.

Now Mr. Gangou may not have been a fan of rock 'n roll, but, like any good agent, he could recognise a gold mine when he saw one. He approached the boys afterwards, and said that he 'quite liked the act' and if they made a test recording he would take it along to a recording manager he knew.

The test recording set them back six pounds they could ill afford. They recorded two rock 'n roll numbers, 'Breathless' (and it was, too!) and 'Lawdy Miss Clawdy'. Cliff proudly played it over to his mother and father, who by now were considerable connoisseurs of rock 'n roll. Their opinion—'a dreadful noise'—came as a bit of a blow.

But the opinion of Mr. and Mrs. Webb was not, on this occasion, the crucial one. George Gangou played the disc, presumably decided it reproduced pretty faithfully the mixture that had had such a devastating effect in the Gaumont cinema, and sent it to Norrie Paramor, the recording manager for Columbia. He sent another test recording, of an aspiring operatic singer, at the same time. When Mr. Paramor phoned to say that he liked the record, George Gangou thought he was referring to the budding Caruso. Mercifully for Cliff and the others—the would-be English Elvis was at that moment trying hard but unsuccessfully to concentrate on a pile of tedious forms in the offices of Ferguson radio—they knew nothing of this. At any rate, Norrie Paramor eventually made it clear that it was Cliff Richard and the Drifters in whom he was interested. He would like to meet them and hear them play, and he fixed with George a date for them to visit his office with their instruments and equipment.

The problem facing Norrie Paramor at that time was common to all involved in the production of pop music. The rock 'n roll boom was at flood-tide, most of the top performers being American. Every hopeful young singer or group, and every sharp operator, was struggling to get on to the band-wagon: it was not easy to tell them apart. Obviously fame and fortune awaited any British singer and group who could reproduce the genuine thing, but recording managers know that in the ephemeral world of pop a great deal of money can be lost by backing the 'easy-money' performer rather than the potential professional who will give value for money. In short, he wanted to be sure that any group he promoted in this field were not just in it for a quick and easy return, but were genuine performers anxious to make the grade.

From his first contact with the Drifters, when Cliff nervously opened the door of his office and said, 'I'm here!' Mr. Paramor's fears that he was dealing with slick operators were dispersed.

'Very soon,' he recalls, 'the boys had rigged up their electric guitars and drums, and my office became drenched in a whirlwind of rock 'n roll. It was good and loud, with the emphasis on both.' Cliff and the Drifters passed their audition, but the agony of indecision for them was not yet resolved. Norrie Paramor told them that he would like them to make a record, but that he was going away for a fortnight's holiday and would be in touch with them again when he got back.

It may have been a fortnight's holiday for Columbia's recording manager, but it was fourteen days of torture for the Drifters. During the evenings they would go over the events of the previous few weeks in great detail, and plan for the days ahead when they would be famous. But when Cliff got to bed at night in the Cheshunt council house he had known since he was ten, the realities of the present took over. Did he really expect that a boy from the estate could be famous like Elvis? Did he dare to imagine that he, of all people, could be a real top performer? Surely they had rushed things a bit ... bitten off more than they could chew? They should have practised more, worked harder.

Things were not helped by the fact that direct comparisons were easily made. He would play an Elvis record, and then compare it with their test record. Nothing made him despair more profoundly. Presley was so good, so polished and assured. They were terrible: noisy and awful.

All sorts of doubts arose. Supposing Mr. Paramor came back from holiday and forgot all about them? Supposing while he was away and had a chance to think he had changed his mind and dropped the whole idea of their making a record? The possibilities were too ghastly to contemplate.

Cliff's girl friend—he had a regular one at the time—found the fortnight very trying. They would be out walking and she would be chatting away ... but getting no response at all. He would be in a world of his own. His parents, too, found things touchy, and only the tremendous sense of family unity, forged in the hard days of the recent past, kept at bay bad temper and squabbling.

When at last Mr. Paramor did send for them, they had almost convinced themselves it was to tell them that he had changed his mind about the record. In fact, he simply told them that he had a song he would like Cliff to record, but he was not too sure about the group. Although he saw the value of maintaining the unit, he also doubted whether performers who could not read a note of music could cope with recording a completely new song.

Cliff argued for the group, and the group did their best to look confident, and in the end it was agreed that Cliff Richard and the Drifters should record, as their first-ever disc, a song called 'Schoolboy Crush'.

One minor problem was that records have two sides, and Norrie Paramor had no suggestion as to what could back 'Schoolboy Crush'. The answer came with startling rapidity. On the way home to Cheshunt in the Green Line bus, Ian Samwell, who had a fast-developing flair for this sort of thing, roughed out the words and a theme for a rock 'n roll number called 'Move It'.

Raw beginners at this sort of thing, the Drifters reported to the recording studios a week or so later. After further discussion about the backing, Mr. Paramor had arranged for two 'session men'—seasoned professional musicians—to join the group for the recording. They were Frank Clarke (bass) and Ernie Shear (lead guitar), and anybody listening attentively to the record will soon discern how vital a part they played in the sound produced. For hours they worked until Mr. Paramor was satisfied. Then, in an atmosphere tense with care and longing, they recorded the two songs.

The boys were a little disheartened to learn that it would be a month or so before the record was in the shops. They had rather hoped for overnight fame. But at least the deed was done. 'Schoolboy Crush', with 'Move It'—in one of the worst pieces of transatlantic jargon—on the 'flip-side', was in the can. Not one note of it could be changed now, for better or worse.

While they were waiting for the record to be released, George Gangou got in touch with Cliff, to say that he had got a booking for him to do a four-week season at Butlin's Holiday Camp, Clacton.

'What do you mean—me?' Cliff queried. 'What about the group?'

George was sorry, but Butlin's only wanted the soloist. Cliff dug his heels in.

'Unless you book the group, you don't get me.'

He argued that without the Drifters he would be only half as effective. He offered to take a smaller fee if the boys could be included as well. When George saw that he was adamant, he went back to Butlin's to plead their cause, and won. Cliff Richard and the Drifters were signed on to perform at Butlin's for the princely fee of nine pounds a week each, plus free board.

Since returning to England from India, Cliff had never had a holiday by the sea. But now he was not only off to the seaside with his friends, but being paid to do it.

Obviously this four-week engagement put paid to his job at Ferguson's. Not as reluctantly as he ought to have done, probably, he went to his boss and gave in his notice.

'You're a nice boy, Harry,' he said. 'But I'm not sorry to see you go. You never were cut out to be a clerk.'

On August 9th, 1958, just before leaving for Butlin's, Cliff Richard signed a long-term contract and became a professional. The boy from Cheshunt was most emphatically on the way up at last.

## CHAPTER IV

## SHORT CUT TO THE TOP

AUGUST 1958 at Butlin's Holiday Camp, Clacton, was quite a memorable month, especially for the Drifters. They could hardly contemplate a more idyllic operation than lying in the sun listening to their own, brand new, just released record being played over 'Radio Butlin'.

'And now, campers,' the metallic voice over the Tannoy would say, 'here is "Move It" by our very own Cliff Richard and the Drifters, who play for you every morning and evening in the Rock 'n Roll Ballroom.'

The very announcement was music enough!

The sessions were exciting, too. For some strange managerial reason they were first asked to perform in the Jolly Roger, which was a sort of bogus pub. However, the beat led to a teen-age invasion; staid men sipping their mild and bitter were seen so far to forget themselves as to bang their pint-pots rhythmically on the counter, and business rather fell away in the general confusion.

Consultations took place at high level, and the boys were asked to transfer to the South Sea Music Bar.

Here the peace and tranquillity of pseudo Hawaii was rudely disturbed by a more raucous kind of electric guitar, and again a move was discussed. At last, five days after their first performance, the boys arrived where they felt most at home—in the Rock 'n Roll Ballroom. Here, for hundreds of teen-agers, the more orthodox delights of candy floss, big dipper and the bathing pool were neglected for the big beat. For a couple of hours in the morning, and a couple more each evening, Cliff and his colleagues more than earned their nine pounds a week.

Back in London, too, things were moving. The B.B.C. was awoken to the fact that rock 'n roll was sweeping the land, with a beat show called 6.5 *Special*, the creation of a gifted producer, Jack Good. Now the independent channel wanted to produce a rival show, even more pacy and lively than 6.5 *Special*. To achieve it, they first lured Good away from the B.B.C., and then asked him to produce a programme in the beat idiom for 'younger viewers', which would make the B.B.C. show look antique.

Good was a graduate of Oxford University, former lead with the Oxford University Dramatic Society, and in every outward way a 'high-brow'. At school he had turned in a magnificent performance (for a seventeen-year-old) as Othello, and everybody predicted a great future for him as an actor or drama producer.

In fact, he had turned his eyes towards television. Always a man of his time, intensely contemporary, he had seen where others in television had not, the way in which the current pop music could be visualised and presented as first-class screen entertainment. During that August 1958 Jack Good was planning Britain's first truly visual pop music TV show, to be called *Oh Boy!* It would include groups and soloists, settings and lights, dancers and movement. The camera would cut quickly from scene to scene in time with the beat, switching from dancing feet to groping hands, from blaring brass to dancing shadows. It was the sort of show that not long before people would have said was impossible to present on television. But Jack Good was a single-minded, persistent man. He had seen the possibility, and it *would* be done.

He had a colourful jazz organist, Cherry Wainer, and a highly original group of instrumentalists sporting the gorgeous title Lord Rockingham's XI. What he lacked was a new star singer, someone who could be coached and moulded from the start into this new, highly sophisticated medium.

Norrie Paramor knew of this project, and suggested to Franklin Boyd, whose firm had published the music of 'Schoolboy Crush', that he should pay a visit to Jack Good and play him Cliff's record.

Good listened attentively to both sides. After a moment's thought he said, in typically forthright fashion, that he did not care much for 'Schoolboy Crush', but he liked 'Move It'.

'Who is Cliff Richard's manager?' he enquired.

That was quite a tricky question, because he did not have one. Johnny Foster had done the job up till now, but already he was confessing that he was out of his depth. Clearly the time had come for a change. Norrie Paramor was consulted and suggested Franklin Boyd, and for ten months he acted as Cliff's personal manager. Almost his first job was to sign him up for a regular spot in the new *Oh Boy!* show.

By now—towards the end of the Butlin season— Cliff's very first record was moving into the charts: those statistical assessors of popularity. It had just entered the Top Twenty—a remarkable feat for a record by an unknown artist and group. But it was not for the 'A' side ('Schoolboy Crush') that people were buying it, but for the 'B' side, the 'filler' composed on a Green Line bus, 'Move It'.

Listening to the two records now, with hindsight, it is not hard to see why. 'Schoolboy Crush' is a trivial, corny piece, in a rather raw Presley style, about calf love, with an insistent plea that 'this is not just a schoolboy crush'. It was a record written, one guesses, by a market researcher, purpose-built to appeal to schoolgirls, without much in the way of originality or flair to commend it.

'Move It', on the other hand, is exciting. It is pure, primitive rock 'n roll. It builds up in the traditional way: a few sharp chords from the lead guitar, then the whole thing is transferred to its rhythmic foundation, an insistent, vibrating bottom E on the electric bass, which, apart from half a dozen B's in the central section, is plugged relentlessly all through. Upon this foundation the drums and rhythm guitar build the fast, pulsing tempo of rock 'n roll, the lead guitar links the vocal sections, and the voice, inescapably young, tops the whole thing with its emotional appeal.

Rock 'n roll singing was a new style, caught rather than taught. In 'Move It', for instance, the voice for the most part is hovering around middle C, but the whole technique is the introduction of sudden trills or runs above or below the basic note, and, in this case, dropping a full fifth quite unexpectedly at the end of a passage. The words spill out at a tremendous rate, and the total effect is of irresistible momentum: hence doubtless the clapping, stamping and near-hysteria induced by the music in so many of its hearers. Listen to 'Move It' a few times and you feel in the grip of a relentless stream of sound, to which something very basic and probably primitive in the human nature responds.

The words of 'Move It' are not very important. They add up to a hymn of praise to rock 'n roll—'the rhythm that gets into your heart and soul, let me tell you, baby, it's called rock 'n roll.' In passing it pours scorn on ballads and calypso in comparison with country music 'which just drives along.'

Cliff has undoubtedly produced many technically better records, but it is hard to think of one since that first ever to surpass it for sheer impact. Nothing, in the climate of 1958, could have been better calculated to launch a new star: and yet, as we have seen, it was almost an accident, the first published composition of a part-time guitarist in an unknown semi-professional group.

*Oh Boy!* confirmed the instant appeal, not only of 'Move It' (which finally got to No. 2 in the Hit Parade) but also of Cliff himself. At first Jack Good insisted on Cliff's appearing without the Drifters, backed by Lord Rockingham's XI. Later, when their relative market values had somewhat changed, Cliff was able to insist that his own group should accompany him.

A period of hectic activity followed, in those first few weeks of the autumn of 1958. A stage tour of one-night stands were booked, there were regular TV appearances, approaches were made about Cliff's appearing in a film, and there were more records to be made.

About now a letter came to Cliff's Cheshunt home. It was in answer to his application two years ago to appear in Hughie Green's *Opportunity Knocks,* and offered him a chance to appear in the television talent spotting show. However, on this occasion Opportunity Knocked too late: not for Cliff, but for Mr. Green, as it happened.

The stage tour was sensational. Cliff and the Drifters were engaged to support the Kalin Twins, an American pair whose record was currently top of the Hit Parade.

Just as the tour was to begin, Ken Pavey, who had been booked as the Drifter's leading guitarist (a position which had never been permanently filled) pulled out, for domestic reasons. John Foster went down to the 21's to see if he could find a replacement. He asked around, and his attention was drawn to a thin Geordie with glasses, called Hank Marvin. He heard him play, and on the spot offered him the job. But there was a snag.

Hank was insisting on a package deal. If he joined up, his pal Bruce Welch must come too. Could he play the Drifters' style of music? Hank assured John that he could—and then disappeared with Bruce to their digs and spent the night learning it and practising all Cliff's numbers. Hank and Bruce, of course, became the longest-serving members of the group.

Cliff and the Drifters were getting two hundred pounds for the fortnight's tour—not exactly super-tax class divided between five of them, but better money than any of them had ever earned before. While they were on that tour a guitarist called Jet Harris, who was with another act called The Most Brothers, stood in with the Drifters for some items as an extra instrumentalist, and after the tour joined them permanently, replacing Ian Samwell, who wanted to concentrate on writing songs (and achieved considerable success, composing several of Cliff's early successes).

But the sensations on the tour were not connected with these back-stage rearrangements. The Kalin Twins began the tour as the stars, and Cliff and the Drifters were programme fillers. The Twins had their record 'When?' at the top of the charts; Cliff's record was just in the Top Twenty.

By the end of the tour the whole situation had

changed. The audiences were screaming for Cliff and ignoring the Americans. Cliff's record had gone above 'When?' in the charts. Cliff and the Drifters were the first item after the interval, allegedly to pave the way for the Kalin Twins. But the audience would not let them leave the stage. The Twins never got on stage on time. At some places the whole audience went wild. On the night when Cliff celebrated his eighteenth birthday, the show had to stop while the fans sang 'Happy birthday to you'.

Incidentally, it was during this tour that Cliff managed to travel by bus without feeling sick for the first time in his memory; and he has never felt sick on a bus since.

It was this tour, 'Move It' and *Oh Boy!* that put Cliff and the Drifters into the limelight. From the point of view of stage presentation, he probably owes more to Jack Good and *Oh Boy!* than anybody.

Good's technique in this respect was unusual, to say the least. He assured Cliff, at their very first meeting—outside Leicester Square tube station—that he would teach him how to appear without a guitar.

'I shan't know what to do with my hands!' Cliff objected.

Jack Good's answer was to make Cliff rehearse his songs seated sedately in a chair, hands folded on his lap, then, slowly, as the singer caught the mood of the song, to introduce this or that gesture or movement, naturally, as part of its expression. He would show him how to look into the correct camera, and how to avoid unnatural or exaggerated gestures.

At about the same time, and again on Jack Good's insistence, Cliff shaved off his Presley-type sideburns. After all, Good explained, he was going to cultivate a 'mean' look, in the Presley manner, on the show, and the two together would look like a ludicrous carbon of the American star.

In fact, it came hard to Cliff to stop being Presley's double. It was, of course, a sure-fire route to quick success; but it was also the way to a brief and un-memorable career. For months the Presley manner-isms persisted—and, of course, the 'mean' look. Cliff's present comment, after seeing some of the early *Oh Boy!* shows re-screened privately, was that he had never seen anything so gormless in his life.

In fact, it was Cliff's appearance and movements on stage in *Oh Boy!* that brought the first serious Press attack on him.

It came in a couple of daily papers, including the *Daily Mirror*, and in the pop paper, *New Musical Express*. The attack was specific and strong. Cliff was accused of 'crude exhibitionism' on an *Oh Boy!* show in December 1958. His 'violent hip-swinging' during 'an obvious attempt to copy Elvis Presley' was 're-volting . . .' a 'form of indecency.'

'If we are expected,' the *NME* column continued, 'to believe that Cliff Richard was acting "naturally", then consideration for medical treatment before it's too late may be advisable.

'While firmly believing that Cliff Richard can

emerge into a top star and enjoy a lengthy musical
career, it will only be accomplished by dispensing with
short-sighted, vulgar tactics.'

Looking back on this attack eight years later, Cliff
still feels it was rather unfair. 'There is a narrow
borderline,' he says, 'between reasonable rhythmical
movement and what is ridiculous or indecent. If
movements and gyrations have an element of choreo-
graphy—if they really express visually what the song
is saying in words—then they are surely all right. But
when the singer goes all out to paw all over the stage
and make suggestive body movements—and I agree
some have done this—then that is obviously wrong.

'I can honestly say I cannot remember ever going
out on stage to try to be sexy. Some of it was pretty
wild, some of it was pretty gormless, but I thought
then, and so did my parents, incidentally, and I still
feel now, that it was not indecent or vulgar.'

This was the period of the rock 'n roll riots, and
understandably writers and commentators were very
sensitive to anything on stage that seemed calculated
to spark off violence. There seems little doubt that an
insistent strong beat does erode a sense of responsibility, in much the same way as alcohol does; but,
while that might lead to screaming and even stamping,
there is no evidence that it can lead emotionally
normal people to do things—like engage in physical
violence or promiscuity—contrary to their normal
behaviour.

The rock 'n roll riots, in Cliff's view, were not

caused by music, but rock 'n roll concerts were the occasion of them. There is plenty of evidence that gangs of fifty to a hundred young men would turn up at concerts with the express intention of having a riot whatever happened. For some reason, possibly jealousy, a number of London gangs seemed to take a particular dislike to Cliff and the Drifters and twice in the London area broke up his shows during that first winter of his career.

The first time was at the Trocadero, scene of Cliff's earlier humiliation over the talent contest. He and the Drifters had been warned that fifty or so gang members from the East End were openly boasting that they would break up the show. Sure enough, as soon as it came to the Drifters' turn and they were nicely focused in the spotlights, a fusillade of missiles bombarded the stage. It was remarkable that none of them was hurt, but a flying penny—a vicious missile —knocked a sizeable piece of wood out of a guitar, and the stage was quickly littered with coins and other projectiles.

That occasion was bad, but a week or two later at the Lyceum, just off the Strand, was even worse. The Press had given big publicity to the Trocadero rioting, which served to advertise the idea to any other lay-abouts and roughnecks who were looking for a plausible excuse for a bundle. The announcement of a week's stage show at the Lyceum, only a couple of miles away, must have seemed to the yobs a glorious opportunity for a repeat performance, and so it was.

The Lyceum was jam-packed for the first night, standing room only. The presentation included a revolving stage, and Cliff and the Drifters were due to make their first appearance on it, slowly revolving into sight playing their opening number. As the stage came round and they appeared to the view of half the audience, and when they had barely played four or five bars, the first incident occured. Thrown with deadly accuracy from the rear stalls by an unseen hand, a buttered bun flew over the footlights and thudded soggily into the drums.

That was the signal for a barrage of projectiles. People in the audience got hit, and not unnaturally stood up to remonstrate with the missile launchers. Private fights broke out, girls screamed, somebody switched on the house lights and the stage manager pushed a button and revolved Cliff and the group, still only half-way through their first number, out of sight. Now whatever else was the cause, rock 'n roll, heat or bodily contortions on stage could not be blamed for *that* riot. It was clearly planned and premeditated.

Scenes of chaos ensued. The police were called, hysterical young girls who had paid good pocket money to see the show were rescued from the midst of a vicious brawl in the auditorium, running fights broke out all down the Strand between rival gangs.

When the last Black Maria had made its way back to the police station and the damage could be assessed it was decided to call off the rest of the week's shows. It would have been necessary anyway, because the emotional turmoil of that evening had made Cliff lose his voice. He has always had a 'nervous' throat—his voice often goes husky just before a show—and the sight of this unbelievable chaos at one of his shows brought on a sort of paralysis of the voice muscles. A doctor ordered him not to sing a note for a week.

One of Cliff's office staff recalls that one night when there had been violent and ugly scenes outside a theatre where he was appearing she saw him sit down in the dressing room and cover his face with his hands in shame and embarrassment.

One such bad occasion was at the Chiswick Empire. Word came down to the dressing room that things were pretty bad. The audience had got a little rowdy and had started throwing things. Cliff sensed they were warming up for his personal appearance. As the moments passed things grew worse, and when it was time to go on Cliff turned to the Drifters and said, 'Let's go fellows, after all, they can't kill us.' A shower of eggs, tomatoes and vegetables of all descriptions met them as they launched into their first number and the music was almost drowned by the noise from the gallery. Within seconds the stage looked like a miniature Covent Garden. Throughout it all Cliff and the boys kept on playing. A girl sitting in the stalls was hit by a heavy fire extinguisher which had been thrown down from the gallery.

On another occasion, at Romford, there was a tremendous crowd outside. Hundreds had been locked out, and there was a great deal of pushing and shoving, and inside the theatre it was quite hectic. The crowd was screaming, 'We want Cliff, we want Cliff.' The coach was brought right up to the stage door, and when the crowd outside realised they would catch only a glimpse of Cliff, there was a howl and a breaking of glass. A brick had been thrown through one of the coach windows. After the show, for more than an hour, everybody stayed besieged inside. At intervals there would be another crash of breaking glass as young toughs flung more bricks. Finally the police were called and gave protection. When the time at last came for Cliff to leave there was a terrific howling from the crowd, but under cover of protection from the police they managed to get into their transport without serious damage.

Strangely enough, after some fairly stiff sentences by magistrates, rock 'n roll riots slowly died out. Fans continued to scream, of course, and clap and stamp. But the vicious rioting at beat shows was replaced by riots at the seaside between Mods and Rockers and, more recently still, by riots going to and returning from football matches. It seems that the occasion is not the cause, after all.

During this early period, when Cliff was enjoying a meteoric rise to fame, he changed managers. This is not a very common occurrence, and led to some unpleasant Press comment at the time.

Franklin Boyd, who became his manager from the time Cliff signed on for *Oh Boy!*, was a music publisher first and foremost. He seemed to conceive of the manager's task as being to find as many engagements as possible for his artist.

The result was very nearly disastrous. For a while, everybody wanted Cliff. Rock 'n roll stars used to last about six months, so the feeling was that it was important to cash in quickly with a new star before his inevitable fall from the firmament. TV and radio, personal appearances, a film, press interviews, recording sessions—all came tumbling in on the bewildered young eighteen-year-old singer.

The climax came in one awful week. During it Cliff did the *Oh Boy!* show, together with its rehearsals; made daily visits to the film studios where they were shooting *Serious Charge*, in which he had a small but important role; appeared on the Jack Jackson TV show, and, to cap it all, was appearing *every night* in a week's variety at the Finsbury Park Empire. Any one of those engagements would ideally constitute a week's reasonable work!

By the Saturday night Cliff was exhausted. He crawled home and fell into bed. He slept through the alarm the next morning, and when his mother woke him to remind him he was due at rehearsals, he broke down.

'I can't stand this life any more,' he complained bitterly. 'I'd sooner go back to my old job in the factory if this is what it's going to be like.'

His father's reaction was drastic, but, in the circumstances, justified. He wrote to Franklin Boyd and terminated his engagement as Cliff's manager. Then they turned to Norrie Paramor for advice.

What had happened where Franklin Boyd was concerned was simply that the speed of events surrounding Cliff overwhelmed him. He was a generous and friendly man who had done a great deal to launch the new star, but if a manager's job includes seeing that the artist only undertakes such engagements as he can adequately fulfil, then he was not succeeding.

Mr. Paramor confirmed an opinion expressed to Cliff by Cherry Wainer, the organist in *Oh Boy!*, that her manager, Tito Burns, was an experienced and wise one. So a meeting was arranged, and a contract signed between Cliff's father (Cliff not yet being 21) and Tito Burns, which would expire on the singer's twenty-first birthday.

Tito Burns' vast experience of show business, and of handling performers, managements and producers, proved invaluable, and there was no repetition of the blackest week in Cliff's career under his guidance.

The next major turning point in Cliff's career came with the making of the film *Serious Charge*. The way in which he came to be offered a part in it is a story in itself.

Lionel Bart, later to be the composer of many highly popular musical comedy scores, had met Cliff on one occasion at Cheshunt, and had followed the young man's sudden flight to fame with interest. After completing a score for a musical during a long hibernation in Cornwall, Bart came up to town to consider an offer to write the music for a new film,

*Serious Charge*, which was to star Andrew Ray, Anthony Quayle and Sarah Churchill. He had studied the treatment, and agreed to work on the music. The film included a part for a young singer, and Bart's publisher asked him if he had any suggestions for the role.

Lionel Bart remembered the young man from Cheshunt, now hitting the headlines and the TV screens, and suggested Cliff. The idea was passed on to the producer of the film, and Cliff was given a camera test at Elstree studios. His television technique, so carefully taught by Jack Good, stood him in good stead, and he was given the part.

The film (which concerned a 'serious charge' made by a youth club member against a parson—it earned an 'X' certificate) and Cliff's share in it, were mainly important for him because of one song, 'Living Doll'. When he first heard it, he did not like it; and it was not improved for him by being accompanied in the film by a group engaged by the studios. However, an E.P. record had to be made of the songs from the film, and for this Cliff was able to use the Drifters. At his own suggestion they took it much slower than in the film, and the result was a record that sold over a million copies and topped the hit parade for six weeks. For this, Cliff was awarded one of the coveted 'Golden Discs'. This record marked an important advance in Cliff's career for another reason. It was not a rock 'n roll number. 'Living Doll' was the polished, fairly sophisticated kind of country and Western ballad that was a thousand miles beyond the reach of the run-of-the-mill beat soloist. It was the first definite sign that Cliff might have a career as an entertainer that would survive the numbered days of the rock.

The Drifters had a new drummer by now. Terry Smart, the sole survivor of the old Cheshunt days, was good enough for everything but the really top class. Now that they were operating at that level, his minor deficiencies began to be a little more obvious. It was Terry himself who took the next step, telling Cliff that he had always wanted to join the Merchant Navy (which was true) and that now seemed the right time to do so. Tony Meehan, a small sixteen-year-old who exuded confidence and had played the drums almost from his cradle, took Terry's place and brought real flair to the rhythm side of the group.

They also got a new name. In 1959 news filtered back from the United States that there was a group there named The Drifters. The Americans had the name first, and with Cliff's records now beginning to sell overseas it was obvious that confusion must be avoided and the name of the British group changed. The inevitable debate about a new name followed—and changing the name of an established group is a tricky step. But the one chosen was so obviously right—The Shadows—that it was immediately accepted by everybody.

A second film followed very shortly for Cliff, and it was this one that made his mark as a film personality. Called *Expresso Bongo* and written by a highly literate and rather cynical playwright, Wolf Mankowitz, it was in fact an exposé of the pop music business. It tells the story of a young singer who is discovered bashing bongos in an expresso coffee bar, and is taken up by an unscrupulous agent, put over to the public with all the calculated cunning of the mass manipulator, and shamelessly exploited. 'Bongo' Herbert, as he is known, becomes an overnight sensation, launching a new craze—the bongos—and enjoying the wild adulation of the fans. He comes complete with the right sort of image. Bongo Herbert loves his Mum (in fact he hates her). Bongo Herbert is a religious boy who goes to church each Sunday (in fact he thinks it is all a big joke). Behind the façade of the clear-eyed, talented youngster is the reality of a young man slowly being corrupted by success; until the novice who was exploited by his manager becomes the star who doublecrosses his inventor. The great Charing Cross Road creation has become a Frankenstein's monster, beyond the control of his creator.

Many critics and film-goers assumed that Cliff as Bongo Herbert was more or less playing himself. In fact, as we have seen, the two characters are poles apart, except for their sudden rise to fame. Cliff was not being exploited, his public image was and is very much his private one, too, and his fame was not dependent on a passing craze like the bongos.

But Cliff could really get inside this character. After reading the script he only insisted on one change. As originally written, Bongo Herbert was even insincere about his own enjoyment of the music he was singing. Cliff felt he could not possibly sing the two or three songs in the film 'insincerely'—partly because it would be beyond his acting ability, and partly because the one thing that lifted his own treatment of rock 'n roll above the average was his sheer enjoyment of it and involvement in it.

With that difficulty settled, Cliff enjoyed playing the part. It was concerned, after all, with a world he knew well—the world of Tin Pan Alley, of smart disc-jockeys, of scheming agents and unscrupulous ad-men who knew every trick in the business of extracting money from the pockets of the newly-rich teen-agers. Apart from the final twist (in which Herbert turns on his exploiters) Cliff felt the story was sufficiently true to life to have honesty and relevance.

Whatever the reason, he turned in a first-class performance, which earned him unexpected praise from Val Guest, the film's director-producer : 'Cliff will be an even greater success as an actor than he is now as a singer.'

*Expresso Bongo* was a good film by any standards, and enjoyed a tremendous success. One of Cliff's songs in it—a ballad, 'Voice in the Wilderness'—reached No. 2 in the hit parade.

It would probably have reached the top spot but for a bad error of judgement by Cliff himself. Cliff was not enthusiastic about the song—rock 'n roll was still his first love—and all along he had felt that the 'B' side, 'Don't be mad at me', was the better number on the record and would be more popular than 'Voice in the Wilderness'.

Just before leaving for his first tour in Canada and the United States, he was invited to record three songs for the B.B.C. radio show *Top of the Pops*. Although 'Voice in the Wilderness' was by then in the Top Twenty and climbing, Cliff decided to record the 'B' side instead. If Tito Burns had been there he would have objected, but he did not arrive until Cliff had finished.

Tito asked what he had recorded. Cliff told him.

'And what about "Voice in the Wilderness"?'

'Oh, I don't like that song. I gave it a miss,' was the reply.

Tito Burns began to lay down the law about plugging 'A' sides, and Cliff responded by explaining that he was the singer, that he preferred 'Don't be mad at me', and that no one, manager, agent or recording company, could do anything about it.

The unedifying scene ended with Burns exclaiming 'You know it all now—why pay me?' and walking off. Cliff had the sense to run after him and apologise, and the incident was temporarily forgotten.

However, while they were in the States they heard that 'Voice in the Wilderness' was second in the hit parade.

'Do you think it will get to number one?' Cliff asked Tito.

'With a good plug on the radio just now it might,' Burns commented.

Cliff agreed.

'Those *Top of the Pops* programmes will be being broadcast about now, won't they?' the manager pointed out. 'Now you see why I wanted you to record "Voice in the Wilderness".'

It was a sharp lesson for Cliff, and the only time he has had a serious difference with his personal manager. It also reflects a really significant trait in Cliff's character. The very determination and single-mindedness which helped him to the top could manifest itself as obstinacy on occasions. Once he made up his mind about anything, it was exceedingly difficult to make him change it; though maturity has brought a great flexibility and willingness to change his mind.

In fact, 'Voice in the Wilderness' is a delightful record. Apart from the words, which are unconvincingly sentimental, it is the sort of lyrical ballad with which Cliff achieved so many successes later in his career, and, for this author at least, would figure among a favourite half-dozen of his records.

*Expresso Bongo* and records like 'Voice in the Wilderness' really marked the end of the rock 'n roll phase for Cliff Richard. He has always continued to sing some 'up-tempo' numbers, but earlier than most he and his advisers saw the decline of rock 'n roll as a phase in popular music history, and decided (in the business phrase) to 'diversify his interests'. The gradual transformation of Cliff Richard and the Drifters—raw, exciting and adolescent rock 'n rollers

—into Cliff Richard and the Shadows, polished, confident all-round entertainers, was one of the most fascinating things in the show business world of the early 1960s.

## CHAPTER V

# THE ERA OF ROCK

IT would be wrong to leave the rock 'n roll era without taking a closer look at a rock 'n roll stage show. True, it was television, radio and records that made a man a national figure and his name (however briefly) a household word. But it was the stage show and the one-night stand, complete with screaming girls, stampedes and hysteria, that was the elemental heart of the thing.

Part of the appeal, as Cliff was well aware from his own schooldays, was the anticipation of it. Unlike playgoers making their way to a West End first night, the fans knew exactly what they were going to hear: they had already worn the performer's records thin and probably knew the lyrics better than he did. On the other hand, they were not like concert goers making their way to a philharmonic concert in the Festival Hall, where the audience knows the music it is to hear, but goes for the sake of the performance. The audience at a rock 'n roll show was not very bothered by the performance: indeed, such was the din that they normally could not tell whether the performance was good, bad or indifferent. One newspaper critic,

sent to review a Cliff Richard show at the Chiswick
Empire, wrote: 'How do you review an act in which
it's practically impossible to hear a single word? . . . I
don't think I've ever heard such an ear-splitting
barrage of sound as that which greeted Cliff's appearance and which accompanied him throughout his
half-hour on stage.'

The fans expected this. They were not paying good
money to hear the same numbers that they could ex-
tract endlessly from their record players at home, but
for an experience. As the crowds gathered outside the
theatre or hall—groups of girls in sweaters and casual
skirts or jeans, a few girls with their boy friends, and a
few knots of boys on their own—the emotional build-
up began. The queueing to get in, the rush for the
best seats, the besieging of the car in which Cliff
arrived : all of this was part of the occasion.

So were the preliminaries in the show—the hapless
minor acts whose main purpose was to increase the
sense of impatient expectancy for the top of the bill.

Back-stage, Cliff and the group would be assem-
bling their equipment, checking on entries and order
of items, and getting dressed. Part of a rock 'n roll
presentation was the singer's appearance. Cliff's taste
was fairly exotic: a black shirt, perhaps, with a pink
jacket and trousers and Italian shoes. His dark hair
would be immaculate at the start of the act, but after a
few bars it would begin to assume a carefully stage-
managed kind of disorder. Such details could not be
left to chance.

At last the minor acts would be through, and the big curtain, shrouding the top of the bill performers from the auditorium, would be the only thing between a thousand fans—hearts in mouths—and the main act. There would be a moment's dramatic pause, a hush, and then the curtain would sweep up to reveal the group in place, poised, ready. Suddenly a clean, electric chord starts a dynamo of sound, another curtain parts, and Cliff runs on stage, trailing mike in hand, picked up by the main spotlight.

The theatre explodes. Even the opening bars of the first number are drowned in the noise. They know what it is going to be, anyway, but in some mysterious way the slim figure on the stage acts as a catalyst for all the pent-up expectancy and emotion. His stance on stage is provocative, flamboyant, almost aggressive: knees slightly bent, leaning backwards, swaying to the beat, almost defying the audience to engulf him in sound.

As the beat begins to penetrate the noise—and little beyond it can be heard—so the singer becomes, as Cliff has himself expressed it, a sort of transmitter, conveying in stance and gesture and dance steps (and, when they can hear it, in words) the heart of what the group's music is trying to say.

A tremendous empathy builds up between the singer and fans. They respond to his presence on stage; he responds to their presence in the theatre. It is no longer Cliff's show, but theirs.

'I reckon,' Cliff says, 'that screaming was as much a

part of rock 'n roll as the drums were. A rock 'n roll show without a scream would have been pretty boring.'

At some stage in the show, in those early days, it usually got beyond just screaming. Anyone who has studied the face of a young teen-age girl screaming at her pop star will appreciate that this is utter dedication, not so much to a person (after all, they do not *know* him at all) but to a fantasy, an image of all that they worship as ideal and unattainably romantic.

Suddenly, often, something would snap for one of them, and a weeping, screaming girl would push out of the stalls, run up the aisles and clamber on to the stage. It was precisely then that fantasy and real worlds collided. All of a sudden she was up there, alone, lit by the floodlights and within touching distance of Cliff and the group—and she did not know what to do next. The stage looked, from the stalls, like a distant, elusive paradise of light and sound, inhabited by demi-gods. But from the stage it looked like a lonely, noisy plateau of creaking planks and hardboard sets: and the demi-gods were perspiring young guitarists not basically very different from the young men in the youth clubs.

'But . . . you're *ordinary*!'

Cliff never failed to be amused when a fan who has finally got through the barriers and had a chance to talk to him lets slip her honest assessment of the erstwhile idol.

Usually the excitement grows. On one occasion the

last number of the act was 'A Whole Lot of Shaking' and the crowd, Jet Harris related in a magazine interview, was really rocking.

'Their reaction was so strong that we could hardly hear ourselves playing. Towards the end of this number Cliff crouched down and almost embraced the microphone. He sank lower and lower on to his knees still whispering, the light dimmed and he was left picked out alone by a brilliant spotlight. Suddenly Cliff leapt to his feet, crying "One more time!" The music grew louder and faster, the lights came on again as he spun round. That was when the audience really let themselves go. Uniformed attendants stood around the stage to stop people climbing up to touch Cliff. The audience was really in a frenzy and so were we. When the final chord was struck, the roar of the crowd was like a football match at Wembley, and when Cliff ran on for another curtain there was an even bigger roar. As he was leaving the stage there was a commotion among the crowd. Two girls holding hands had jumped from the balcony on to the stage. This was not so terrifying as it sounds, as the balcony was quite low and near the stage. Anyway, the escapade was in vain as Cliff had disappeared into the wings.'

For the majority who stayed in their seats the magic half-hour came and went. The applause swelled, the cheering and shouting, the appeals to the artists not to leave them; and then the final curtain fell; they wiped away the tears and dispersed to the coffee bars and clubs and five hundred front parlours to live it over again in recollection. Pity the unwise parent who tried to join in *that* conversation.

'You don't understand, Mum, it's no use trying.'

Rock 'n roll was the badge of being a teen-ager in the late fifties, and they jealously guarded its mysteries from the adult world. Of course many older people enjoyed it (and it could be very enjoyable), but it was more than entertainment to the youngsters—it was a way of life, a sign of rebellion, an instrument of power.

Many adults wondered whether the screaming and hysteria were harmful. There were dire warnings about the aphrodisiac qualities of beat music, and about the nameless orgies into which erotic stage gyrations and gestures might lure innocent youngsters. Time has given the lie to most of them.

Of course, as performers like Cliff were quick to admit, there were rock 'n roll groups and singers who crossed the borders of good taste. Possibly at times— so slender is the line dividing—even the most blameless performers were unconsciously erotic. But who can tell where sexual instinct is, and is not, at work in any human activity?

In any case, the great majority of the screaming girls had not yet reached puberty. Most of them were twelve or thirteen years old. Older fans did not scream—one fan wrote to Cliff, 'Now I'm fifteen I find I don't want to scream any more.' It is hard to imagine that sex, in the normal sense, played much part in this.

Perhaps more subtle is the whole notion of 'being sent'. The phrase is descriptive. 'Even on stage I can get "sent",' says Cliff. 'For one moment the Shadows "get through" to me and I'm "gone"—but only for a second. Only people who are mentally weak already could be disturbed by it.'

Undoubtedly one of the chief appeals of rock was just here: its ability to get beyond reason and sense, and touch some primitive nerve of ecstasy. All powerful, rhythmic music is capable of this, including of course, a number of works in the regular repertoires of symphony orchestras. (The rhythmic structure of Cliff's 'Move It' is almost identical with that of the 'Ritual Fire Dance'.) Whether it is morally good or evil seems an unanswerable question. Possibly, like many other instinctive sensations, it is morally neutral, but capable of evil exploitation in the hands of the unscrupulous.

So far as one can tell the vast majority of British youngsters emerged morally and emotionally unscathed from the era of rock 'n roll. They survived it, and moved on into motherhood, or business, or homebuilding. Cliff, almost alone among the great rock 'n rollers of the fifties, also survived it, and moved on unscathed into a different sort of career, and a different sort of dedication, as well.

## CHAPTER VI

# THE MAKING OF A STAR

BY mid-1961 it was obvious that Cliff Richard had come to stay as a major figure in the entertainment world. He had behind him sixteen records, every one of which had been in the hit parade—twelve of them in the number one or two spots. During 1960 his name had appeared in the Top Twenty charts for fifty of the fifty-two weeks. He had earned two Golden Discs, for records selling over a million copies. He had done a six-month session at the London Palladium in the show *Stars in Your Eyes*. He had made three pictures, the latest, *The Young Ones*, being widely regarded as the first outstanding British-made musical. It seemed that everything he touched turned to gold. Far from his popularity waning as rock 'n roll slipped into history, he was demonstrably more popular than ever.

This seems the right moment, then, to ask the question, What made Cliff Richard a star?

Perhaps one must decide what constitutes a star in the show business world. After all, it is a modern word of imprecise meaning. There were great actors and vaudeville artists before Hollywood coined the word, but it was the moving picture business that started calling them by this rather flamboyant title.

In Hollywood a film star was an artist who could do what the stars in the sky do—shine. Against a background of lesser lights, the star is meant to sparkle, to stand out as somebody special and distinctive. Taken in this way, the word is quite a vivid one. Many a poor show or dull set has been transformed by a single performer's star qualities. He or she has lifted the whole thing out of mediocrity by an ability to shine, to infuse sparkle and distinction. A star is not necessarily more talented, in the technical sense, than the other performers, but he must have flair, personality and self-confidence.

There were literally hundreds of rock 'n roll singers and groups in 1958, yet out of the ruck emerged this one young man to survive a series of changes in public taste and to be still one of the most popular and highest paid entertainers in the land nine years later.

Cliff Richard as a person is fairly uncomplicated. Although born in India, he is culturally and socially very much a product of the London suburbs. He has the Londoner's quick brain and ready wit, his urbanity and confidence. His accent—despite the effects of Anglo-Indian origin and mid-Atlantic coaching—owes more to Cheshunt than anywhere else. His tastes in clothes, interior furnishings, cars—and even music, privately—are those of middle-brow subtopia. He is not a Cockney, like Tommy Steele, but he is a Londoner: not the London of Bow Bells, but of

Penge, Hounslow, Woodford—and Cheshunt.

As one who has breathed this very air since childhood, the author considers this environment an excellent one to equip a person for life in modern Britain. The suburbs are not beautiful, its people are not exotic characters from Dickens or Bart, its tastes are not high and mighty, nor are they vulgar and earthy. But they *are* real, true to the times. If you want to capture the reality about Britain, you will not go to Aldgate, Lime Street or the Gorbals, but to the suburbs of London, Liverpool or Glasgow, where the ordinary, flesh-and-blood, roast beef and two veg. man-in-the-street Briton lives. Cheshunt, surely, is as near to the heart of fifty million Britains as anywhere in the land. If you know what makes Cheshunt tick—its supermarkets, its secondary schools, its council and private estates—you also know what makes modern Britain tick.

Cliff, then, knows the people. From the start of his career, and with very few miscalculations, he has correctly assessed the mood, tastes and wants of the customers. That is an important ingredient for a modern star.

So is determination: and Cliff has that. Possibly because life for the Webbs had been so hard, and from quite a young age he had had to shoulder responsibilities and share in reaching decisions, Cliff developed early on an absolute determination to succeed. So vital is this dedication, in itself, that should Cliff have had no voice or flair for rhythm, one feels he would have been a star footballer. The fact that, in a life dominated from early teens by pop music, he was still able to earn a county junior cap at soccer shows this quality of determination.

For him, ambition did not mean lying in bed on a Saturday morning constructing a dream world of hit records, fast cars and large cheques. It meant endless practice, driving enthusiasm, and hour upon hour of financially ill-rewarded grind in dance halls and bars. Some writers have implied that his rise to the top was a fluke of fortune. Maybe the circumstances of the rise were lucky, but there was no fluke about the rise itself. There is nothing fluky about three hours of guitar chord practice a night. There is nothing fluky about hauling half a hundredweight of equipment around on buses to entertain local clubs. There is nothing fluky about denying oneself all sorts of minor luxuries in order to finance a chosen career. Ambition is made of sterner stuff than chance.

A good deal of this determination was inherited, doubtless, for the way his parents faced life—the decision to leave India, grappling with adjustment to a new land, father struggling to find a reasonable job, unemployment and disappointment—shows a good measure of determination and fortitude in the face of enormous difficulties. His upbringing equipped him superbly for coping with the fickle world of pop music, where high success can be followed in a matter of weeks by disastrous failure, for this was the family's own experience during his critical formative years.

His mother tells how, when she went into his room in the morning in the early days of his success, he would say to her, 'Pinch me hard, Mum. Is it real?'

'I can't believe it's all happening,' he once said to his secretary. 'I often think I'll wake up some morning and find I've just been dreaming.'

But normally he accepted his good fortune with equanimity. The Webb family history had taught him to treat success and failure, not as 'the same' (a fatuous notion), but as incidental to the real and lasting things —home, relationship, love, being yourself.

Equally, in a family like the Webbs, there was no room for a swollen head. Even today the family takes big brother's success with remarkable calmness. Cliff's father, especially, had a shrewd eye for the dangers of pride for a young man suddenly offered the admiration, bordering on worship, of thousands of fans. The family has always been so close that ostentation or a swollen head on Cliff's part would have been instantly recognised and ridiculed.

The result is that Cliff has always been known as 'the modest star'. He affects no airs, is completely unspoilt and natural, and takes success and praise in his stride. Of course, such things are regularly said in the biographies of living stars, but the fact remains that they are true, and can be verified by everyone who knows Cliff well or has worked with him.

Colin Clewes, an A.T.V. producer who had not worked with Cliff for six years since his early days, was surprised to find him unspoilt: 'One thing was

First night – the telegrams from fans

Celebration with a Maori concert party during New Zealand tour

A recording session for TV in Germany – with Shadows Bruce Welch (guitar) and Brian Bennett (drums)

In thoughtful mood – Cliff spends a quiet few minutes
during a hectic Scandinavian tour

Sightseeing in Paris with Hank Marvin of the Shadows –
Notre Dame in the background

Wherever Cliff goes, the inescapable autograph books appear – even before he's off the plane

Cliff relaxes with the inevitable cup of tea in his West End office

Cliff during rehearsals for the 1968 Eurovision Song Contest, with his backing group, The Ladybirds

*The Voice* in a more serious role – Cliff at Billy Graham's Crusade
at Earls Court

certainly the same, and that is Cliff himself. He hasn't changed in the least as a person, which is another pleasant surprise in this business.'

However, one must make clear what this does *not* imply. It would be quite incorrect to say that Cliff did not enjoy success, or respond to praise. He is modest in the sense of having no grandiose ideas of himself, but not in the other dictionary sense of 'retiring, bashful, having a humble estimate of one's own merits'. He is certainly not bashful nowadays, and his estimate of his own merits is not humble : realistic would be the word. He knows when he has done well, and enjoys being praised for it. He knows when he has not done well, and deplores it. But in all these things he is artless, ingenuous and open. It is this that gives him his deserved reputation for modesty. The opinion of those who knew him as Harry Webb and know him now is that he has not changed in character at all : that is a remarkable tribute.

But while a suitable social and family background, determination, and honest openness are all good factors, they do not add up to a star. The three vital qualities here, where Cliff is concerned, are his voice, his looks, and his personality.

Cliff's voice is light baritone to tenor in pitch, comfortable in the octave below middle E. Within that range, and a few tones on either side of it, it is flexible and accurate. In effect he has two voices. His 'ballad' voice is soft and confidential, lingering over certain phrases and employing an occasional glissando with great effect. The crooner's trick of making the hearer wait for the expected note while he toys with the one above or below it, has been regularly employed by Cliff since his first song in the ballad idiom ('Steady With You').

On the other hand, his 'beat' voice is full-throated, exciting and spontaneous. Like the great jazz singers, he appears to improvise runs and inserts ejaculations and shouts in response to the music itself. In the early rock 'n roll numbers the pace of the performance added to the magnetism, the voice throwing out words and phrases in a steady stream while the backing rocked and rolled along.

There is also a quality of clarity about Cliff's voice: you can actually follow the lyrics, and it retains today a remarkably youthful quality of tone.

Perhaps the best way to describe it is by saying that his voice is likeable, warm and engaging. Without great range of tone or pitch, it is still a *performer's* voice, an excellent medium for expressing mood or emotion.

Cliff's looks have been the subject of female admiration since his schooldays, so we need not spend very long on them. He is, of course, extremely good-looking, in a dark, boyish way. His eyes are alert and expressive, and a vaguely Mediterranean look is strengthened by his slightly dark, very fine skin.

More important in Cliff's career than facial features, however, has been his natural ease of movement. Sitting in a chair, standing, walking, swimming or playing games, one can immediately pick him out as lithe and graceful. This is a tremendous asset on stage. No matter what ridiculous poses he struck in the early days, he always managed to give them a certain distinction and line. When one adds to this ease of movement a natural sense of rhythm, there is the raw material of a dancer; and on stage and in films, in recent years, Cliff has come over very effectively in song and dance routines.

Yet when all is said and done it is 'personality' that makes a star: those distinctive characteristics and qualities of humanity which are his alone. There is an indefinable something about the star that eludes the merely very talented; and whatever that something is, Cliff has got it.

The author has had the advantage of knowing Cliff well as a person before being exposed to him as a stage personality. The latter—the 'stage' Cliff—is a sort of extension or intensification of the former. In a room full of people one immediately picks him out, not just for his good looks or his confidence and ease of manner, but for his ability instantly to relate to people. Cliff gives people his undivided attention, and gets it from them. He can establish in a matter of seconds an easy sympathy (in the correct sense of the word) with almost anybody.

Transfer this ability to relate, this immediate empathy, from a lounge to the stage of the London Palladium, and one has stardom. Cliff on stage is able to establish a *rapport* with the audience—whatever their age or background, the world round—which becomes a bridge over which his own friendliness and sincere joy in what he is doing communicates to them.

So he can bounce on stage in the Palladium panto-mime, jump into an up-tempo dance routine, grin with delight at the audience: and from then on do almost as he likes with them. B. A. Young wrote in the *Financial Times* of Cliff in that show: 'He is as artlessly lovable as ever. It would be absurd to pretend that he has talent on the scale of the panto stars of old . . . But he has remarkable personal magnetism; and if he is in the Palladium panto in thirty years' time, playing the Dame, I hope to be near the front of the first-night queue.'

'Remarkable personal magnetism' just about sums it up. Hank Marvin, one of the Shadows, says, 'Cliff has certainly got some magic, although he probably can't analyse it himself.' It is this, more than anything else, that has turned an overnight hero of rock 'n rollers into a national entertainment star of the first rank.

Just in case anybody thinks that for this reason per-forming comes easily to Cliff, it is worth putting on record that he is one of the world's most nervous artists—before he gets on stage. Waiting in the wings he will shuffle his feet, keep touching his hair, and clear his throat incessantly, right up to the moment when he goes on stage. This nervous tension seems to be essential to a good performance on his part, but even familiarity with a role will not completely al-leviate it.

Equally, he is always sincerely appreciative of approval and praise. One would have thought that the applause of the audience were enough, but to be told as he comes off stage that the act was 'really great' clearly takes a great load off Cliff's mind. It is hard to reconcile this apparent doubt about his own ability with his overwhelming confidence on stage, but in fact they are just two sides of the same character. He knows whether he has done well or badly, but, because he is anxious to please, and to establish a happy *entente* with his audience, he wants to know that they are pleased, too.

On the other hand, Cliff is very sensitive to criticism; probably too sensitive. He has not had to face very much, but obviously it hurts him deeply. Cliff's mother admits, 'I think he knows that in show business you've got to be criticised, but still, I don't think he likes it. I think that is a weak point with him.'

Cliff still smoulders, for instance, at a review which appeared in a Rhodesian paper some years ago of a one-night stand he and the Shadows did in Bulawayo. The writer, over a pen-name, Thespian, tore Cliff's performance to shreds. He described him as utterly without talent or merit. On the other hand, he argued, the Shadows were as talented as Cliff was feeble. The critic ignored the audience's wild enthusiasm for the whole show!

Cliff was shaken to the core by this onslaught, and all the way on the journey down to South Africa he was upset and on edge. Only some highly successful shows—and fulsome reviews—in that country restored his spirits.

'No, I don't like criticism,' Cliff admits, 'especially if it's personal. And I have once or twice suffered—not recently, but in the early days—from really bad mis-reporting.'

One example of this was over the subject of the Trocadero and Lyceum riots, when a reporter inveigled himself into Cliff's London flat, where his mother was looking after him as he recovered from the after-effects. Ostensibly sympathetic, the reporter chatted informally with Cliff and Mrs. Webb, and then went back to Fleet Street to write an unpleasant piece about Cliff being scared of the rioters and 'running back to mummy'.

On the whole, however, Cliff has had an excellent press, partly because he is a good subject for an interview. He likes talking, and enthuses pleasantly on any subject that is currently taking his fancy. Possibly this accounts for the miles of newsprint, and acres of photographs, dedicated to him in the popular press and the teen-ager and music papers. His 'exclusive' interviews are rather a pitfall for journalists, however, as Cliff's views on ephemeral matters change rapidly and such fatuous (but frequently posed) questions as 'what is your favourite drink?' or 'which is your favourite colour?' tend to get different answers each time they are asked. On one occasion two rival magazines for teen-age girls produced 'exclusive' interviews, one headed 'Cliff talks about Love 'n

Marriage' and the other 'Cliff opens his heart about LOVE and MARRIAGE'. Unfortunately, the second of the two to appear was also labelled 'For the first time ever'!

Probably arising from his roots among 'ordinary' people, Cliff has shown in his career a remarkable adaptability, and undoubtedly this is another factor in the star make-up. A newspaper in 1961 commented on the skilful way in which he adapted his stage presentation for an older audience in a theatre. Both before and since then he has also, of course, adapted his basic stock-in-trade, the song and beat group routine, to such varied media as one-night stands, outdoor shows (in Scandinavia and Africa), TV spectaculars and confidential shows, records, radio (notably on his long-running Luxembourg programme some years ago), the cinema, cabaret (at London's Talk of the Town) and even pantomime.

In many cases, of course, this has involved completely new skills and techniques, including dancing, slapstick comedy, straight acting and even mimicry. He has not, so far, fallen down on one of them; and, while he would be the first to admit he is no Nijinsky or Olivier, he is certainly increasingly competent (to say the least) in drama and dance, two fields in which he has had no formal training.

Something of this, of course, must be ascribed to skilful and wise management and direction at crucial points in his career. Cliff is generous in his praise of Jack Good, for instance, who taught him to feel at home on television; and of Norrie Paramor, who shielded him from a number of blunders in the recording field. His film directors in *Serious Charge* and *Expresso Bongo* also helped him, as did some of the fine established actors who were in those films, to adapt to the strange technique of film acting.

'It's very hard,' Cliff explains, 'doing a scene for a film when you don't know where it comes in the story or how it fits in. It's possible that the cast may not get the whole story until they go to the première. At first I found myself standing on set, when I had nothing to say, gawping at the camera and wondering what was going on.'

Tito Burns, Cliff's first contracted manager, played a big part in getting him firmly launched in show business, and set up several important milestone in his career, including *Expresso Bongo* and *The Young Ones*. He also provided a wise and shrewd knowledge of the show business world at a time when Cliff and his parents were innocents let loose in a jungle.

However, by 1961, when Cliff's contract with Tito was due to expire (on his twenty-first birthday), he felt the time had come for a change of personal manager. It seemed to him that Tito Burns was thinking in terms of a short-term, lucrative career, whereas Cliff was now turning his mind more and more to a long-term career as a mature entertainer.

'I reckon it's fairly easy to make hit records once you've got the formula,' says Cliff. 'You just get a good song, make an interesting sound, and it's there.

But it is up to the individual performer to make something of *himself*—to choose records that will help, not hinder, his long-term prospects. Since quite early on we—the Shads and I—have had a definitely long-term attitude.'

To support this view Cliff instances their refusal, towards the end of 1959, to accept ballroom engagements.

'There was more money in ballrooms—more than in one-night stands—but it was always chaotic. We decided "never again". It was no good for our careers. You can't do an act in a ballroom, and you can't develop as an entertainer.'

The manager Cliff appointed in 1961, Peter Gormley, has stayed with him ever since. Allowing for the fact that managing an established star is comparatively easy, yet still Cliff regards him as the ideal manager.

'When he took over as my manager, he wouldn't take any money for the first twelve months, as he reckoned my engagements were the result of Tito's work, not his. That sort of attitude is pretty rare, I reckon.'

Peter also manages the Shadows, and so it is possible to plan jointly at every level.

Sometimes, of course, even at the peak of a star's career, his manager has agonisingly difficult decisions to make. A recent one concerned a Royal Command Variety performance.

Cliff and the Shadows have done a number of these

prestige shows—Cliff's first 'Royal Command' was back in 1959 as part of an *Oh Boy!* act which sent the staid audience into raptures; and he has done five more since then—but they still regard them as difficult occasions.

'Our stuff is still basically youth music,' as Cliff puts it, 'and we've got to get the numbers over to this rather stiff, mickey-suited audience. Apart from a few lonely screams from the gods, where four or five fans have managed to squeeze in, it's not an audience automatically on our side—it's very pro-ey, too: the audience is packed with show-biz people.'

Before a formal invitation is given to appear in a Royal Command show, an informal approach is made, because it is simply not done to turn down a royal invitation. In 1965 Cliff and the Shadows were approached at the unofficial level about appearing in a 'Focus on Pop' section at the Royal Command show. Peter Gormley strongly advised against. He argued that since pop music had become 'respectable' it had tended to die the death on these sort of shows. Cliff and the Shadows did not want their careers linked permanently with the pop sector, either. On this sort of occasion they would normally use an orchestra as well as the guitars, and employ quite a different approach. So, accepting their manager's advice, they indicated that they would sooner not be invited on this occasion.

A less formal royal occasion that gave Cliff a tremendous thrill was the visit of Princess Margaret and the Earl of Snowdon to the Eton College Mission's Youth Club at Hackney in March 1962. It was the Princess herself who suggested that Cliff Richard should sing, and the Shadows play, at this function.

The *New Musical Express* reported, 'For Cliff it was another triumph, for he emerged the perfect host on this great royal occasion, escorting the Princess around with the ease of an ambassador, which he was—the ambassador of the teen-agers.'

In fact Cliff was suffering with laryngitis at the time, and felt he only croaked his way through 'The Young Ones'. Afterwards, at an informal tea party, Cliff talked with Princess Margaret for half an hour, accepting her advice to inhale Friar's Balsam for his throat, and learning that she was intending to see *The Young Ones* the following week-end.

We have said that Cliff Richard's rise to fame was not a fluke; and that is true. But of course there were moments in it when fate or providence seemed to lend a helping hand. Circumstances at several critical junctures conspired to forward Cliff's ambitions, when they might just as easily have frustrated them.

The chance meeting with Ian Samwell at the 21's was one such moment. It was not so much Ian's role as a lead guitarist during the critical period when they were discovered that was important, as his flair for writing songs that suited Cliff's talents and were tailor-made for the current teen-age tastes as well. Three of Cliff's first nine hits (and two of his first three) were Ian Samwell compositions, and he also wrote three

very effective 'B' sides on other records. The first vital
hit, 'Move It', which was the perfect vehicle for Cliff
and the Drifters at that moment in time, was his work.

Meeting Lionel Bart in Cheshunt, and so being
suggested for a role in *Serious Charge*, was a most
timely happening. It represented the first real break
out of the rut of the screaming rock 'n roller for Cliff.
Until *Serious Charge* and its hit song, 'Living Doll', he
was, in his own words, 'strictly for the birds'.

From the long-term point of view it was distinctly
well met with Hank Marvin and Bruce Welch on the
eve of Cliff's first tour, too. He has never minimised
the importance of the Shadows—of whom these two
gifted musicians were for a long time the musical
inspiration—to his career. 'The Shadows generate the
sound,' he says, 'I tap it.' More than that, the part
these two have played as composers, especially of film
and pantomime scores, has been enormous. Two of
Cliff's biggest hits—'Bachelor Boy' and 'Summer
Holiday—were at least partly Bruce Welch's work,
and the Shadows were responsible for all the splendid
music of *Aladdin, Cinderella* and *Finders Keepers*. Of
the score of *Cinderella*, Philip Hope-Wallace of the
*Guardian* wrote, 'The music by the Shadows is
pleasantly melodious and more effective than I had
expected'—high praise coming from that source! Certainly the delightful song 'In the Country'—
melodious, fresh and inventive—from that pantomime
deserves to become a pop classic: apart from a
horrible grammatical lapse in the lyric, which claims

that the country 'belongs to you and I'!

*What makes Cliff a star, then?* Of all these factors, his own personality must be the most crucial. When one adds to personal magnetism a pleasant and highly emotive voice, a natural ease of movement, an attractive appearance, utter dedication, adaptability, good advice and management and the help at critical moments of young men like Samwell, Marvin and Welch, one has the formula for making a star not only of unusual brilliance, but also of proven durability.

## CHAPTER VII

## LIFE AT THE TOP

To the fan, the life of a star is a remote paradise. To the materialist, it is the satisfying of every real and imagined need. To the cynic, it is a candyfloss world, unreal, empty and fleeting.

But what is it like to the star himself? Few people can really visualise what it is like to achieve an ambition suddenly and completely; to find your face in every paper and on the screen, to hear your voice blaring out of a million transistors, to find yourself recognised and mobbed by admirers every time you set foot outside your home, and, of course, to be earning more money in a week than most people earn in four years.

The human character has an enormous capacity for absorption of and adaptation to changes of environment, but it must be desperately taxed to deal with the sort of change that overtook young Harry Webb in the second half of 1958. In early summer he and his friends were just a suburban gang, hopeful, hardworking and broke. Beyond a small area of inner Hertfordshire, nobody had ever heard of them. By the end of the year Harry had a new name, a new job, a national reputation and an income already to be calculated in terms of hundreds of pounds a week. It is a remarkable tribute to his parents and his own character that Cliff Richard, despite the change of name, remained basically Harry Webb, and that the awful fate which overtook so many over-night stars—breakdown and instant extinction—never seriously looked like happening to him.

The most fundamental difference between a star and the rest of us is not, of course, his income. After all, there are anonymous figures in the world of business who earn every penny as much. The most basic difference is the admiration, the public fame, the fan worship. This is an odd phenomenon, and deserves some analysis.

There have always been celebrities, of course, but the growth of the mass media—and especially films and television—has produced the cult of the star. Whereas before a great actor or singer was known only to those who had the opportunity to see and hear him perform, now the star is seen by millions. Hollywood began it, by building up the image of the super-man or super-woman, to represent the fantasy-ideal of the mass audience. They even invented the modern use of the word *glamour*. To Hollywood this meant the aura of visionary splendour, the projection of a select race of stars who drank, as the representatives of the rest of us, the cup of life to the full and were untouched by all the sordid and squalid realities of life at street level. The ancient root of the word glamour comes from

magic and necromancy; and certainly the old Hollywood stars bewitched their audiences, transporting
them from a world of hunger-marches, general strikes
and the rise of Hitler to a fairyland where every dream
came true and every cloud had a silver lining.

Their successors, in the world of the teen-age
boom, are the pop stars. In the thirties there were
hundreds of movie magazines, carrying to millions of
breakfast tables the tiniest and most trivial details of
the tiniest and most trivial film stars. Their clothes
and diets, their vulgar houses and pretentious swimming pools, their divorces and their marriages were
eagerly devoured by the patrons of the Gaumont, the
Ritz and the Roxy.

Today the movie magazines are a spent force. Only
a handful remain, their circulations reduced to the
core of genuine film-lovers who want to read about
films rather than starry scandal. But the pop papers
have taken over. *Disc*, the *New Musical Express*, the
*Melody Maker* and a long list of more ephemeral
publications cater for exactly the same sort of interest
as the old-time movie magazines. The readers have
changed—now they are mostly teens and early
twenties; and the stars have changed—now they are
the kings and queens of the charts. A whole cultic
language has been evolved, known only to the initiated,
and the position of a favourite star's record in the hit
parade becomes a matter of intense emotional involvement.

As of old, every trivial doing of the stars is recorded. Their views on any subject are eagerly sought. A fantasy world is created in which these towering creatures operate. In an age that has largely rejected worship of God, the oddest deities are exalted and given a fervour of adoration seldom achieved by the most devout religionist.

The fans seem to have an almost supernatural knowledge of their idol's plans and movements, and a nation-wide grapevine seems to operate to disseminate it. Within minutes of Cliff's arrival at a hotel—or even before it—the inevitable knot of young girls will gather, the equally inevitable autograph books at the ready. They know when and where he will appear almost as soon as he does, and, literally, sometimes *before* he does. With some mysterious feminine instinct they know which doors to picket, which hotels to watch, which cars to waylay. When Cliff moved house secretly in 1966 to get away from the fans, they knew his new address and ex-directory telephone number the day he moved in.

From the start of his career Cliff has been on the receiving end of this sort of fan worship. Over the years he has learned to come to terms with it.

'Fan worship to me is a strange and fascinating thing—but I've always kept it apart from me. You have to try to get their feet on the ground ... It's flattering, certainly, but personally I've never got emotionally involved with either the money and the fame or the fans.'

Nobody who has not been on the receiving end of

this phenomenon can realise how extraordinary it is.
Idolatry is too weak a word to describe it. 'You're the
only thing that makes life worth while,' a fan wrote to
Cliff. Others have threatened suicide if he refused to
meet them. Some have got so lost in a fantasy world
that they have really convinced themselves that they
were engaged to him, or that he was about to elope
with them.

Of course, these are the extreme exceptions, the
handful of emotional inadequates who have made him
the obsessive centre of their lives. Among these are the
ones who risk their lives jumping on to the stage or in
front of his car, who defy fire-hoses and police horses
to touch him, and who go to fantastic lengths to be
near him.

Something of this fanaticism (and 'fan' comes from
that very word) is illustrated in a story which is
connected with the fact that Cliff used to wear a
crucifix, given him by John Foster. He took to wearing it when he was about fourteen, though he has been
quoted in a magazine as saying it had no special
significance for him.

There came a night when the fans got out of hand
at Manchester and the police turned the hoses on
them. Cliff watched appalled, very worried that they
might get hurt. The crowds had almost been dispersed
by the water treatment when one girl managed to
break through the cordon and the hoses and rushed
up to Cliff, soaked to the skin, exhausted and hysterical. 'Give me something of yours please,' she

screamed. Cliff, without thinking, tore the chain from his neck and gave her the crucifix, and she gave him a rosary. He kept it for a while and when the news of it got around, dozens of crucifixes, rosaries and religious medallions came to Cliff.

The more ordinary fan is harmless enough. Most of them genuinely enjoy their hero's singing or style of music, and admire him in an exaggerated, but not unhealthy way. Probably the majority of Cliff's fans fall into this category.

A smaller, but noisier group, are emotionally in-fatuated with him—or rather, with his stage image. These are the ones who scream themselves hoarse at stage shows, their eyes full of tears and puppy dog devotion, and hoard thousands of photographs and books full of useless information about every detail of Cliff's life.

Among the sort of things the fans want to know (and are duly told by the teen-age romantic papers) are the names of Cliff's pets, what he has for tea, does he make his own bed, what are his favourite names, what colour is his wall-paper, what sort of girl will he marry, what does he like to drink, does he use an electric shaver, which are his favourite sports and so on.

The reason is fairly obvious. These are the sort of details one needs to know to fit out daydreams with that necessary touch of reality.

Supposing, for example, that you just bumped into Cliff in the street one day (these things *do* happen, you read about them in *Valentine*) and asked him home to tea. And supposing he looked at you ('fresh, young and natural'—that's what he told *Marty* he admired in girls) and smiled and agreed to come. And supposing on the way home in his Thunderbird car (you know its number, the colour of the seats and even what he keeps in the glove box) you suddenly realised that you didn't know what he liked for tea . . . Wouldn't that be *dreadful*? But there's no need to worry, because *Mirabelle* had an article 'If Cliff Richard came to tea . . .' and so you always make sure there is plenty of salad and tea cakes for toasting in the larder.

Now provided the object of all this adulation keeps his head—and especially does not allow himself to take advantage of it—this, too, is completely harmless. If you cannot indulge in a few day-dreams at fourteen what is the point of going through a teen-age phase at all?

But a tremendous responsibility rests on the star, whether he likes it or not. Cliff's fans know that he does not smoke and seldom drinks. They know that he strongly disapproves of sex before marriage. They know he believes that marriage is for life. The influence of their star is, in these respects, good and wholesome. But supposing he were a heavy smoker, an excessive drinker, or was involved in a divorce scandal? The effect on the fans would be bad and unhealthy.

It is hard to imagine that being a fan of Cliff Richard has sent any girl off the rails, though ob-

viously youngsters who are already maladjusted or
emotionally insecure may develop an unhelpful obsession. But if the obsession had not been with Cliff it
would have been with the head prefect, or the man
next door, or a friend's elder brother. Indeed, the
degree of isolation of the sensible pop star from his
fans is the greatest safety factor in this sort of situation.

'Nowadays fans get a little bit too much involved
with artists,' Cliff says, 'and this is bad for them and
for the artist.'

He is amused at the tricks some girls get up to in
order to see him or touch him. One girl had herself
crated up in a wooden box and delivered addressed to
him in his theatre dressing room, labelled, 'Please
open at the end of the first half.' There were some
girls who hid in a dressing room cupboard for three
hours and finally fell out when he opened the door,
more dead than alive.

Beyond the fans is yet another circle of people.
These are the millions of ordinary people who see the
show on television or at the cinema, and have a normal
amount of curiosity about the comings and goings of
the rich and famous. Everyone in the public eye has to
learn to live with this: the stranger in the supermarket
who cannot resist enquiring whether you really are *the*
Cliff Richard, and could you just autograph this card
as their niece will never believe they really met you in
the flesh? The waitress in the restaurant will keep
eyeing you warily, consulting with her colleagues at

the other side of the room, and then returning with the menu and requesting a signature. Everywhere the paper and ball-point pen is produced and the auto-graph—the visible proof of a person-to-person (or rather courtier to king) encounter—is sought. The whole thing serves to make normal social life im-possible and helps to imprison show business per-sonalities in a little West End world where to ask for an autograph would be to concede the isolating fact that one is not a celebrity oneself.

'Holidays are one time when I tend to get a bit short tempered,' Cliff confessed in an interview in *Disc Weekly*. 'I love signing autographs and talking to people, and I'm very grateful that they're interested in me. I don't mind it on holiday either, because nearly always they're all reasonable. But when someone asks me to give them a quick song while I'm signing an autograph I always ask them what they do when they're not on holiday. If they answer they are a typist I ask them to type me a letter on the spot. I hope they get my meaning.'

At times this personality cult can be amusing. Cliff was driving north one wet autumn afternoon with an American film director. Suddenly the engine of his little M.G. saloon cut out, and refused to re-start. The film man opened his umbrella, and the two of them sheltered under it at the side of the road and thumbed the passing traffic.

At last a large lorry drew up. The driver climbed down and asked what was wrong. On being told, he offered to tow the car to the nearest garage, and invited the American to share his cab.

When they arrived at the garage, they were profuse in their thanks to the lorry driver. He refused any payment at all, but stood chatting to them while the fault—a minor one involving a rubber tube—was corrected. Suddenly he looked hard at Cliff, who was wearing glasses and looking a bit rain-swept.

'Wait a minute, aren't you Cliff Richard?'

Cliff modestly admitted that he was.

The driver's face showed amusement and amazement in equal proportions.

'Cor, you wait till I tell my young daughter about this,' he said. Then he frowned. 'But she'll never believe me. Here, can I have an autograph?'

It was small enough payment for his kindness, but he drove off in his lorry contentedly clutching a slip of paper that said, 'I don't know you, but I think your dad is great. Cliff Richard.'

On another occasion Cliff was phoning home from a call box in the provinces. Having no change, he asked the operator if he could reverse the charge.

'Your name, please?'

'Richard.'

A pause. 'Cliff Richard?'

'Er, yes, I'm afraid so.'

There was a muffled sound at the other end of the line, then the operator's voice returned.

'Sing us a song, and then I'll connect your call.'

Cliff protested, but to no avail.

'All the girls are plugged in and listening,' the operator insisted. '*Please*, just a few lines.'

Reluctantly, and feeling every kind of an idiot, Cliff stood in the kiosk and managed a stanza of his current hit. The last lonely note died away. There was silence on the other end of the line.

'O.K.?' he enquired.

An older, crisper voice replied.

'This is the supervisor. Your call is connected now, Mr. Richard.'

Unfortunately, the aura surrounding the star is not always a source of amusement. Cliff complains that the moment he became famous he lost most of his old friends.

'Suddenly they became awkward, withdrawn, as though some invisible barrier had been erected. They couldn't talk sensibly to me . . . pretended they didn't know whether to call me Harry or Cliff. Being well known didn't alter my attitude to them—I value my friends—but it altered their attitude to me, I'm afraid.

'Even our relatives were affected. It's crazy, really, but when Mum would ask them why they hadn't been to see us lately they'd say, "Oh, we felt you wouldn't want to see us now"!'

This isolation of the famous is bad for them as human beings, of course. 'People treat show business artists with awe, but it's not the artist's doing. Most of us don't want it that way,' Cliff says.

For this reason, he is always glad to see the glamour image knocked a little. 'When people say to me,

"Aren't you ordinary!" I'm glad; I don't care how they mean it, but the truth is getting through. Mind you, it shows that they had thought me extraordinary before!'

So show business people tend to keep their friendships in the group.

'I don't know how deeply they think about friendship,' Cliff says, 'Or how much real friendship there is at all in the showbiz world—there's a tendency to throw friendship around a bit, and a lot of insincerity, of course. For me, though, friends are people you can trust . . . friendship like that isn't easily found.'

This sort of situation drove Cliff back into the family. Here, at least, was a secure and unchanging relationship, and he counts it the biggest single factor in keeping him on the rails during the first six or seven years of his career.

That was why it gave him such pleasure, in 1959, to move his mother, father and sisters out of their Cheshunt council house into a fine, detached residence in the smooth suburb of Winchmore Hill. Later, after his father died, they moved into an even grander house—Rookswood—at Nazeing, in Essex.

Apart from his cars, and a rather large wardrobe of clothes, this was Cliff's biggest extravagance—to set up the family in the finest house he could find. Rookswood was a mansion fit for a king, but was actually built for a wealthy banker. From the drawing room—antique furniture, marble-topped tables with gold filigree work, satin cushions, pink Chinese rug—

to his mother's bedroom—complete with private luxury bathroom with silver bath taps—it was entirely in keeping with the popular image of the sort of house a star would live in. In fact, it is almost the only thing Cliff has owned or done that *has* fitted that image.

Cliff's own room at Rookswood was more or less self-contained, and also included a dressing room and bathroom. Hundreds of records filled three tiers of shelves, and a vast, antique, hand-carved oak trunk—shipped from Portugal—filled one corner of the room.

When his mother re-married in 1966 Cliff sold Rookswood, bought his mother and her husband a house of their own choosing and chose for himself a considerably less pretentious residence in Totteridge, where he lives with a friend and his friend's mother.

A villa on the coast in Portugal is another luxury, though in fact the pressures of show business life are so great, and the opportunities for privacy in Britain so limited, that a foreign hide-out becomes almost a necessity of life.

Another necessity of life for the pop singer is the fan club. Cliff has two in Britain, and there are Cliff Richard Fan Clubs in Iceland, Hong Kong, Hungary, America, Australia, New Zealand, Holland, Norway, Sweden, France, Germany, Canada, Malaya, Malta, Africa, Spain, Italy, Denmark, Belgium, Switzerland, Israel, Austria and Finland. The original Cliff Richard Fan Club, which closed down in 1967, came into being in a remarkable way.

For a sixteenth birthday present Jan Vane from

Romford asked her boy friend, Eddy, to take her for the evening to the 21's coffee bar in Soho. They survived an excruciatingly bad skiffle group (Eddy wanted to leave at that stage) but cheered up when a lively, big beat group took the platform. Jan was impressed with them, and found that they were called Harry Webb and the Drifters. She was particularly struck by the soloist, and after they had finished their turn she went up to him and asked for his autograph.

This was just about the first time he had been asked for such a thing, and he gladly obliged. Harry, or Cliff, as we had better call him, and the other boys joined Jan and Eddy for a coffee.

Apparently the group had missed the last Green Line bus back to Cheshunt, so Eddy offered to drive them home in his car. Seven of them squashed into the small saloon, and sang most of the way back to Cheshunt. Jan asked Cliff if he had a fan club. 'No,' he replied, 'and no fans, either.'

On the spot Jan offered to start one, and Cliff and Johnny Foster agreed there and then that she was appointed official fan club secretary. The first member joined in June, one more in July, four in August and then, from the time 'Move It' entered the charts, the club grew at a tremendous rate, reaching ten thousand members in less than a year. At the age of nineteen Cliff was getting five thousand letters a week, and that number subsequently rose even higher. It was a remarkable achievement by a sixteen-year-old girl to organise such a vast operation, but she kept it up for

the best part of nine years, reaching a peak member-
ship of over forty thousand, until marriage and
domestic responsibilities made her give it up.

A great deal of unfair nonsense is talked about fan
clubs. Certainly Jan Vane was highly indignant at an
I.T.V. documentary on the subject in 1965. This
implied that the clubs exploited the fans for commercial ends, making a huge financial profit and
cynically manoeuvring the teen-agers to promote sales
of records, books, jewellery and so on.

Certainly where the Cliff Richard Fan Club is concerned (and this goes for the continuing International
Cliff Richard Fan Club) this is grossly misleading.
Cliff's fan club has sponsored five orphan children in
East Africa, paying for their keep by donations sent in
on Cliff's birthday; collects silver paper to provide
guide dogs for the blind, and foreign and British
stamps for various charities. Having read scores of
issues of their magazine-newsletter, one is forced to the
conclusion that this is a harmless and pleasant enough
outlet for some mild hero-worship and common interest in a certain style of music. Members are urged
to buy Cliff's latest record, of course ('Let's see if we
can make this another number one!'), but most of
them would probably do that anyway. There also
appears to be a ready market for photos of Cliff, and
Cliff Richard lockets, pendants and so on.

Fans can be a problem. Several times the Fan Club
magazine has pleaded with fans to respect Cliff's
privacy at his home at Nazeing in Essex and during

one Blackpool season Jan Vane pleaded: 'Cliff has already had to move house once in Blackpool. If you should manage to find out his address please, *please* don't make a nuisance of yourself. Cliff is used to fans outside his gate at home but, as he put it, his neighbours in Blackpool are there for a holiday and, most likely, a rest, and they are not going to take too kindly to fans unthoughtfully shouting out for Cliff. No doubt many of you will see Cliff on the beach with his family or friends. Just remember he's just like you or me and doesn't feel able to relax with people standing around staring at him. If you should see him and want to ask for his autograph, by all means do so, but then move on and try not to broadcast where he is. I think Cliff deserves all the relaxation he can get. Thanks a million to all members who take note of this.'

Cliff Richard actually failed to attend the première of his own film, *Summer Holiday*, and all because of some of his fans. Cliff drew up outside the Warner Cinema in his Cadillac. The crowd waiting for his arrival broke through the police barrier and descended on the car from all angles. Cliff made two attempts to leave his car but on both occasions he was forced back by the crowd, until finally he was advised by the police to drive on. A very depressed, disappointed Cliff spent the entire evening watching TV at his manager's flat. He delayed his South African tour especially to attend the British première, and the Fan Club magazine secretary wrote, 'I hope all concerned with the riot are thoroughly ashamed of themselves. If only they had all stood still everyone would have got a glimpse of him, but instead nobody saw him and it just serves them right. It is my opinion that at least half the crowd were just passers-by who didn't really know what was happening and so stood around to see.'

One of the things the Fan Club can do from time to time is enable a few members actually to meet the great man himself. In 1964, for instance, there was a raffle (tickets three for one shilling—proceeds towards a fund for African orphans), the lucky winners to have an opportunity to meet Cliff in his dressing room at Blackpool. However, this sort of plan is fraught with complications, as a letter of complaint to the club from a 'lucky' winner demonstrates.

'As another member was going in at nine-twenty I decided I'd go in on my own at six-fifty, as I thought I'd have him to myself for about ten minutes in his dressing room. I took six autograph books for Cliff to sign. I went through the stage door and Cliff was coming down from the stage. He shook hands with me and started to sign the books. I asked him some questions, then he said, "I'll have to go on now", so I shook hands with him again and I kissed him on the cheek.

'Well, if that's the best Cliff can do, or you for that matter, I'm ashamed of you. I'd bought a new outfit for the occasion and had a new hair-style all for nothing. I was only with Cliff for one minute, so, as I've nine minutes still to come, could you write me and tell me when I can see him again?'

On the other hand, most of those fortunate enough to meet Cliff were obviously well pleased: 'A day I shall remember all my life, the day my dreams came true,' wrote one ... 'You will never know how happy you have made me,' wrote another. Other comments were in the same vein: 'Meeting Cliff was the greatest moment in my life ...' 'He really is the nicest person I have ever met ...' 'He's much nicer looking in real life. I can't put into words what a thrill it was to meet him; he is very pleasant and well-mannered and he couldn't have been any nicer.'

One girl gave up her job in Batley (Yorkshire) when she heard of Cliff's season in Blackpool and found a new one near the theatre.

But the most revealing comment came from another raffle winner, who wrote afterwards, 'He just didn't seem like Cliff Richard at all, he was so *normal*!' Nothing could summarise the whole star cult better than that.

The International Cliff Richard Fan Club, run by Pat Burns from her London home, has contacts with Cliff's fans in scores of countries. With the winding down of Jan Vane's club, it may well take over as the principal rallying point for Cliff's British fans as well.

Once or twice the fans have played a crucial part in the choice of a hit record. 'Please Don't Tease', for instance, was not greatly liked by Cliff or his A and R manager, but a panel of fans who were invited to choose his next release from a batch of possibles put this number easily first. It was duly released and reached number one.

There was another unusual circumstance about this record. In autumn 1960, when it was at the top of the Hit Parade, the Shadows' instrumental 'Apache' was number two. What many people did not know was that the four Shadows and Cliff performed on *both* records—the Shadows accompanying Cliff's song, and Cliff playing a Congo drum on the Shadows' instrumental!

On another occasion the fans got a Cliff Richard record which was never released in Britain into the British charts. 'Gee Whiz It's You' was made as a single for overseas markets only (because it was on the L.P. 'Me and My Shadows' in Britain) but the fans discovered one could order overseas releases from the dealers, and bought enough copies to get it into the Top Twenty!

One of the things all the fans are most interested in is Cliff's matrimonial prospects. Answering the question, 'Is Cliff engaged?' the club magazine was cagey: 'No, and he's not thinking of it at present. But we must face up to the fact that one day he's going to get married. After all he's only human.'

This answer was published during the only period of Cliff's career when he really did look like getting married, a fact which Jan Vane must have known. On the other hand, in another issue she appeared to dismiss rumours of a romance (even naming the young lady concerned) by warning readers 'not to believe all they read in the papers.'

The young woman in question was a dancer in the chorus in Cliff's Blackpool show, Jackie Irving, and he went steady with her for three years—'as long as some showbiz marriages,' as Cliff puts it. The 'inner circle' were quite sure that this was it, and that 'bachelor boy' Cliff was heading for the altar.

Cliff even got as far as discussing with his manager, Peter Gormley, the likely effects on his career of a marriage at that stage (1963). Peter agreed with Cliff that it would almost certainly make no difference at all. Cliff's mother was all in favour of his getting married, 'though perhaps she was not exactly all out for Jackie,' and his sisters enthusiastically approved.

Despite the fact that he had known her well for three years (which is about two and a half years above par for 'walking out') and found her good company, attractive and charming, Cliff was not really sure about marriage with Jackie. He had always been one to wrestle with his doubts before making up his mind, and then not change it. Where marriage was concerned, he sincerely believed it was a lifetime commitment, and that meant he really must be sure.

The serious doubts came quite suddenly. Jackie was 'a very nice girl', and in one sense he felt he was 'ready' for marriage. On the other hand, although he had made a vow not to squabble or row with her, squabbles and rows began and multiplied. Usually they were over trivial matters, but the effect on their relationship was not trivial.

At any rate, the doubts came. 'I reckoned doubts were no basis for a marriage, and I broke it off—suddenly and cleanly.'

Jackie is the only girl Cliff has ever dated seriously, which probably demonstrates more than anything the tremendous sublimation that ambition and success provides. The whole incident also shows how Cliff's thinking has been conditioned by his environment. All around him, including some among his closest friends, he has seen apparently happy marriages involving show business people inexplicably break up. His caution is born of a realistic assessment of the difficulties.

'Half of them get married too young,' he says, 'and some look at it in the light that if it doesn't work out well, we'll scrap it and start again. Marriage, for lots of showbiz people, is just another part of living—it doesn't mean anything to them.'

At about the time when he broke with Jackie Irving religion was beginning to become a dominant factor in Cliff's thinking, as we shall see later. This only served to strengthen his already fairly severe views about the sanctity of marriage and the importance of high moral standards on the part of those who are in the public eye. Back in 1960 he was quoted as saying, 'I have the highest of moral codes. That's the way I've been brought up. I don't care whether you think I'm a prude or not because I believe that decent living is more important than anything else in the world. It's important for everyone to conduct themselves decently, but it's even more important for me.'

People naturally tend to associate loose living and lax morals with the show business world. Cliff agrees that standards are more elastic than in ordinary life.

'In the old rock 'n roll days some of the musicians used to go on stage, deliberately select a girl in the audience, and then pick her up after the show. After a beat show, with all the excitement and glamour, it would be quite easy to pick up a girl, but it would be irresponsible.'

He also agrees that many musicians take drugs. 'They think they play good music when they're "high", but in fact they're terrible!'

Today, though, Cliff thinks things are worse than they were eight or nine years ago. 'Lyrics have got much worse, until now some are definitely obscene. It's not going to help youngsters morally . . . pop stars do have a responsibility to their fans.'

Of course, part of this is the fruit of the growing cynicism and sophistication of our society, and can be seen in many other spheres as well. Cliff's songs for the most part, have either been about romantic love, unrequited love, or some gay escapist theme like 'Summer Holiday' or 'In the Country', and most other songs until the mid-sixties were on those sort of subjects.

But more recently there has come an influx of songs with (at first) suggestive and then blatantly and avowedly sexy lyrics. Several of the songs sung by the

Rolling Stones have had crude and suggestive themes, and one well-known group (Dave Dee, Dozy, Beaky, Mick and Tich) have openly admitted that their songs are sexy.

This was in an interview in *Disc* in September 1966. Dave Dee admitted that the group 'deliberately went out of its way to produce a song laden with innuendo,' just as they 'deliberately went out of their way to produce a fairly uninhibited sexy "blue-tinged" performance on stage.'

He described their current record ('Bend It') as 'a sexy song'—'and we're sexy.' 'We found by accident that we had sex appeal and now we've built up everything on that . . . We use sex subtly (on stage) and provoke the audience that way . . . If they want to touch me I'm pleased. They can do what they like, they're our fans.'

At least one can applaud the honesty of these remarks. It is fairly clear that in the general uninhibited atmosphere of the mid-sixties some pop singers and groups have worked out a short cut to evoking a frenzied response by shamelessly exploiting sex, and it does no harm for parents (and fans, for that matter) to know what is going on.

Although standards obviously have loosened recently, Cliff would deny that the show business world is riddled with immorality. 'Sex is a game . . . a farce to many in the entertainment world,' he admits, 'but there are also many who are happily married and steer clear of scandal. That goes for big names and little ones.'

The old Hollywood innuendo was that talentless actresses could get to the top by using sexual bribery. 'I believe it may happen with second-rate performers,' Cliff comments, 'who have no talent to offer. But so far as I can see, sex takes second place to greed in daily life—if they can make money out of you they're not going to miss the chance because of your scruples about sex . . . All I can say for sure is that no one has ever made such propositions to me.'

In case all of this makes Cliff Richard sound too good to be true, perhaps one had better add that he has at different times admitted to being sorely tempted by three of the Seven Deadly Sins—anger, envy and pride. Until fairly recently, although he is basically a placid and composed sort of person, he was capable of sudden bursts of anger, usually sparked off by what he considered to be a 'liberty' taken by somebody. Envy, too, he has admitted, especially at times when he has seen others succeeding in areas where he has not been successful, and, in the old days, before he had begun to succeed.

Pride is rather a strong word for Cliff's third weak point. Vanity describes it better. Although he favours casual clothes and flops around his dressing room in worn slippers and an old red dressing gown as often as not, he is in fact jealous of his personal appearance.

He was rather anxious, for instance, about wearing glasses when performing. Cliff is short-sighted and needs glasses for reading, but he thought they might spoil his appearance.

He came into his office one day looking rather anxious, and told the two girls there that he wanted their opinion. He was appearing on Billy Cotton's TV show that night, and at one point he was required to read from a script. Without his glasses on he simply would not be able to read it.

'What do you think?' he asked, as he put his glasses on.

The girls studied him carefully and said that they really could not see any difference—'they make you look a bit more solemn, that's all.'

'Do you think the fans will mind?' Cliff asked.

The girls could not be sure, but could see no reason why the fans should object.

Cliff was still a little worried, but when it came to the script reading part he slipped his glasses on casually. The following morning there was a flood of letters from fans, nearly all of them very complimentary.

Cliff cannot bear even to think of himself as fat. 'I hated *The Young Ones*,' he says, 'because I was very bad in it—fat and bad.' A more offensive combination could not be found for him. At one time he weighed twelve and a half stone (he is over five feet ten inches tall, so that is not really heavy); now he weighs a mere ten stone, and looks positively lanky. This is the result of a careful diet—saccharin in tea and coffee, crispbread and cheese for lunch, and so on—especially before television appearances.

'A couple of pounds on my weight makes my face look much fatter,' he explains confidentially, 'and it is very noticeable on television. I really starve myself before a TV show.'

In fact, it was because of a TV show—though not one of his—that he first began dieting seriously. It was in 1963—a year after *The Young Ones* was released. Cliff was sitting at home watching *Coronation Street*, and almost died with embarrassment when Minnie Caldwell remarked how much she liked 'that chubby Cliff Richard'.

This vanity extends to clothes, of course. During the first few years of his career Cliff established quite a reputation as a dandy, getting through literally scores of suits and jackets and a hundred or so shirts in a year. His choices of colours were exotic too—pink, gold, wine and yellow mingling with his favourite black shirts and multicoloured socks. Maturity calmed things down a great deal, but still Cliff enjoys choosing and wearing attractive clothes.

For years his favourite possession, however, was his car; and he owned quite a selection of them, mostly fairly sporty. He graduated by way of a Sunbeam Alpine and a Thunderbird to an E-type Jaguar, but prefers a smaller car for running around.

These things, of course, were the recognised trappings of the star. In fact, most of them sat fairly lightly on Cliff. When his first record was a fantastic success, he enjoyed the unrepeatable first rapture of success. 'It was like everything you've ever wanted all happening at once,' he recalls.

But he soon got used to it. 'Within four records we had started asking, "What are the advance sales like?" We had somehow or other lost that tremendous feeling of bewilderment and surprise.'

It was much the same with money. Like many others from a background where every penny has had to be watched, Cliff has never believed in throwing money around. It was, of course, a wonderful feeling suddenly having enough of it to do many of the things he had always wanted to do—buy his parents a house, get a fast car, have a Continental holiday—but it always hurt him if he found he had wasted it. He was quite indignant, for instance, after one of his first visits to a night club to find he had spent more in one evening than his father earned in a week.

'I don't love money,' he once said, 'but everybody likes it . . . it's money that makes the world go round. I don't sing for the money, in fact, I never ask how much I earn for anything. Singing is just a marvellous thing that I love doing.'

Cliff literally does not know today how rich he is. An accountant watches his investments and shares, and pays his personal bills. He also arranges Cliff's personal pocket money, which now stands at around £15 a week. Press reports that he is a millionaire are dismissed by Cliff as guesswork. 'If I don't know, how can they?'

He does own a vast block of shares in Constellation Songs, one of the companies launched by a group of entertainers to capitalise on their current success. But nobody can estimate what their market value would drop to if Cliff pulled out! However, he is certainly very rich by any standards; but he is telling the truth when he says he has very little 'love of riches'. He is just as happy living in a suburban semi-detached in Finchley—which he did, for choice, for six months in 1965—as in a palatial residence like Rookswood. Indeed, one feels he would nowadays want to add, 'much happier'. The life of a rich man has truly begun to lose its appeal.

In fact, that could be said about the whole notion of life as a star for the mature Cliff Richard. As we shall see in a later chapter, other interests and concerns began to penetrate his thinking from 1962 onwards, and one effect of this spiritual fifth column was to open his eyes to the tawdriness of much that surrounded him, and the pointlessness, in ultimate terms, of the show business rat race.

In the winter of 1964–5, for instance, he told George Rooney in an interview in *Music Echo*, 'For me personally it's a lot of fun, but sometimes I get fed up with everything . . . You tend to feel that life isn't your own any more . . . In the last year or so I've gained a new frame of mind . . . If I really get to dislike it I shall leave immediately.'

It is worth noting in passing that those words were spoken by a young man of twenty-four during an outstandingly successful pantomime run at the London Palladium, and were published the week his record,

'The Minute You're Gone', reached the top of the Hit Parade. These views contrast violently with those he held earlier in his career, and show how different this 'new frame of mind' was: 'After that first tour, I knew there would never be any other life for me ... It's hard work, but it's fun, doing what we like best in the world ... It's great sitting on top of the world. It's more fun being a success than a failure ... and any-way you can have a better time because successful people earn more money!' So spoke the Cliff Richard of 1960.

Money enabled Cliff to indulge in a great variety of sports and hobbies—horse-riding, badminton and photography among them—but one feels that his pattern of life today would be much the same, rich or poor.

The quality that gives Cliff his natural enjoyment of life, and makes him such an excellent companion, is the one delightfully analysed by former Shadows drummer, Tony Meehan, who was quoted in a *Woman's Own* article as insisting that Cliff is basically a romantic person. 'By that, he didn't mean anything to do with falling in love ... Cliff saw the world as a romantic place where beautiful and romantic things could happen.' That is exactly right, and one can underline it from personal observation. Cliff *is* a romantic (as one might expect), though in recent years his religious convictions have tinged the romanticism with a strong dose of realism. He has the romantic's urgent desire to see the best in everyone and everything, and the romantic's slightly pathetic tenderness to criticism. He really does want to see everybody happy—his mother's report after a return visit to his boyhood area in India profoundly depressed him: the poverty, disease and suffering she described appalled him. Part of growing up for Cliff Richard has been the painful necessity of learning the reality of evil and pain and their presence just below the surface of even a sunshine life like his. Possibly the first serious step towards this maturity was the death of his father in 1961, as we shall see later.

## CHAPTER VIII

## ALL THE WORLD'S A STAGE

FROM 1962 onwards Cliff Richard's show business career took wings. He became the first really international British star in his field, he turned his hand to stage shows, more and better films and even intimate revue.

His overseas successes were remarkable. Until Cliff's appearance on the scene the world pop market was the footstool of the Americans. Yet in 1963 the top American show business magazine *Billboard,* analysing the pop charts of thirty-four nations outside the U.S.A., found that Cliff Richard was the world's biggest international star. Elvis Presley was second and the Shadows—incredibly—were third. In May of that year records by Cliff Richard were numbers one, two and three in the Canadian hit parade—'Bachelor Boy', 'Summer Holiday' and 'Dancing Shoes'. A record that reached the number two spot in Britain that autumn—'It's All in the Game'—topped the charts in Hong Kong, Israel, New Zealand, Canada and half a dozen countries in Europe.

In case it is considered surprising that there is a hit parade in places like Hong Kong, one might add here that Cliff has achieved very big sales in Thailand, and that Prince Farook Ahamat of Colombo was once a fully paid-up member of his fan club!

Cliff has had tremendous receptions in countries all over the world. In Scandinavia football grounds were booked for his shows because the theatres would not have been big enough for the crowds. His one night appearance at the Paris Olympia in 1963 was sensational, the management squeezing two thousand five hundred people into a two thousand seat theatre. Cliff reckons he has never been so well received anywhere. As a surprise he ended the show with 'La Mer' in French, and brought the house down. The cheering and applause lasted for five minutes after the final curtain.

In fact, France is his favourite country as a performer. 'The audiences are perfect,' he says. 'They listen in dead silence during the song, and then explode with enthusiasm after it's finished. That's real appreciation.'

Interestingly enough, Cliff does not notice a great deal of difference in audience reaction to his shows from one country, or even continent, to another.

'Pop music and beat is universal,' he considers. 'We get almost exactly the same reaction everywhere.'

Cliff was involved in one or two Continental copies of the rock 'n roll riots, the worst one being in Kiel, Germany. As the performers locked themselves in the dressing rooms the fans went wild in the corridors and auditorium. The police decided to use hoses and smoke bombs to clear the building, but the effect of these tactics was to cause panic among the hysterical girls jammed tight in the corridors. As others pushed into the passages to get away from the smoke and water, the situation began to look really unpleasant. However, order was restored and Cliff and the Shadows were rescued from their dressing rooms. Never again would they believe that the Germans are phlegmatic and coldly disciplined.

Cliff and the Shadows have twice visited South Africa—in 1962 and 1964—and both times were amazed at the reception, with thousands of fans thronging the airport and car hooters sounding a real presidential welcome. 'South Africa has everything in its favour, except *apartheid*,' Cliff says. As the Musicians Union and Equity have agreed on a ban on British members performing in the Republic, as a protest against South Africa's racial policies, there is no possibility of Cliff paying another visit there.

In one way he feels this is a pity. 'I would whole-heartedly approve of the ban if I honestly thought it would help to end *apartheid*, but it seems to me rather a pointless gesture. This way nobody—black, white or coloured—gets a chance to see the act.

'The first time we went to South Africa they had only arranged shows for whites. We weren't happy about this, so we offered to do shows free for the Bantu and coloured people, and in fact we did one in each town we went to.

'I want to stress this,' Cliff adds, 'We are against

*apartheid*—all of us. That is why we want to entertain everybody, no matter what colour their skin. But it seems to me South Africa will have to be changed from within—I don't think we are going to be able to force them by these sort of bans to change their ways.'

Cliff and the Shadows have also performed to mixed audiences of Europeans and Africans in Kenya and Rhodesia, and behind the Iron Curtain in Poland, where they enrolled scores of members for the Fan Club.

That led to an unusual complication. It is not possible for individuals in Eastern Europe to send money to Britain, so the Polish youngsters could not pay the five shillings enrolment fee. To overcome the difficulty, British fans 'adopted' the ones from Poland —and other Communist countries—and paid their fees for them. Cliff was not able to take any money out of Poland, either, so the modest fee he received was spent on souvenirs of his visit!

With all this world-wide acclaim, it is a remarkable fact that Cliff's records have not sold well in the United States. He has been there five times, and has been very popular on stage and television—forty million watched him on the Ed Sullivan show in 1964 —but even in recent years when records by British artists have been right to the top of the American hit parade, his have got nowhere at all.

It would seem that the Americans know of him (some of them at least!) as an entertainer—he has been seven times on the Ed Sullivan show—but not as a recording artist.

One of Cliff's American tours coincided with the Cuba missiles crisis. He was touring in the South at the height of the tension and found people were not very interested in music just then.

'Everybody was rushing about buying up tinned food and packed lunches and so on, and then taking to their fall-out shelters . . . It was fantastic. Tanks patrolled the streets. About sixty people turned up at our show in an auditorium that could seat a thousand!'

Cliff recalls that when the crisis was over people found themselves with eight months' supply of food on their hands, but the shops were not going to buy it back from them!

Although Cliff did not like himself in *The Young Ones*, it seems that almost everybody else did. At any rate, from the time of that film onwards it was widely recognised that Cliff Richard was a major figure in the film as well as the pop world. According to a survey by the *New York Motion Picture Herald* covering two thousand three hundred British cinemas, Cliff was the top box office draw in Britain during 1963.

*The Young Ones* was a winner from the start. Its story and music made it a picture for the teen-agers, who in the early sixties were very conscious of their group identity within society. Yet the *Evening News* said, 'It would be a tragedy if only teen-agers were to see this film.' Andy Gray described it as 'the best musical Britain had ever made and the finest teen-age screen entertainment produced for a long time any-where.'

The story is calculated to appeal to younger cinema-goers. Cliff plays the part of Nicky, a young beat singer who belongs to an informal youth club meeting in a dilapidated hut in Paddington. His father (played by Robert Morley) is a rich property owner who has plans to demolish the hut and build an office block on the site. Nicky has never told his friends of his father's identity, but his father learns that he is a member of the youth club that stands between him and a highly lucrative deal.

The plot consists of a running battle between the club members, who are trying to raise enough money to buy the lease of their site, and the property owner, who is determined to stop them. There is a good deal of coming and going and dark conspiracy before finally father relents and promises to build the young-sters a new youth club.

The music in the film was lively and tuneful, the dancing was choreographed by the American Herbert Ross (who arranged the dance sequences in *Carmen Jones*) and the photography, in CinemaScope, was excellent. There was every ingredient of a hit there, and it turned out to be one.

*The Young Ones* made Cliff's name as a cinema box office draw, but *Summer Holiday* made his reputation as a film star. One critic wrote, 'As a musical, *Summer Holiday* is probably the best British effort to have ever been produced. As a film it is wonderfully enjoyable and entertaining.'

Artistically it is streets ahead of *The Young Ones*. Shot on location in Greece, the film includes much captivating photography. It also has two of Cliff's most popular songs—'Bachelor Boy' and 'Summer Holiday'. The latter, a delightfully gay and cheerful song, may well prove as durable as 'White Christmas'. Certainly it was still being played on the radio during the holiday season four years after the film's release, which is very unusual for a pop record.

The production numbers and dance sequences were again choreographed by Herbert Ross, but whereas Cliff merely essayed a few steps in *The Young Ones*, this time he danced expertly through these scenes. Ross commented at the time that Cliff's dancing had progressed wonderfully since *The Young Ones*.

The film itself is, of course, about a summer holiday. Its opening sequence is brilliant. A typical British summer day—pouring with rain—is shown in black and white. But as the red London bus which is to take a crowd of youngsters on holiday, drives into the picture the whole scene turns into brilliant colour.

*Summer Holiday* earned more money than any British musical film up to that time, playing to packed houses all over Britain and Europe. For Cliff it was another milestone. As impresario Leslie Grade said in the *Daily Mirror*, 'What you must not forget is that Cliff has developed tremendously as an actor. After all, Cliff is a talented, contented boy who loves his work. I remember there were people who said he wouldn't last five minutes, but he's been a big star for six years. Groups come and groups go, because it is not the hardest thing in show business to make a star. The hardest thing is to make a star stay a star, and Cliff's films have helped to do this.'

It was quite true that people had predicted when Cliff first came on the scene that he would not last. 'He'll be just another runner in the pop stakes,' wrote one critic, while others offered scorn, sympathy or cold comfort: 'He'll never make it. It takes a lot of talent, and where is his?' 'He's got to fight against some of the best singers in the pop business it'll be tough going . . .' 'Nobody can be this country's top pop singer, there are too many already.'

That was in 1959, but even in 1962, while *Summer Holiday* was being filmed, the cynics were still doubting Cliff's staying power. He had to learn to drive a bus for his part in the film, and a radio announcer reported that London Transport had offered to give Cliff a job as a bus driver whenever he needed one. The announcer could not resist adding, 'And knowing exactly how long pop stars last, in probably two years' time Cliff will have to take them at their word.'

In fact, *four* years later—in 1966—Cliff was still voted Top British Male Singer in the annual N.M.E. poll, an honour he had received for five consecutive years! There is little doubt, as Leslie Grade said, that Cliff's films have been a major factor in keeping him at the top, and none of them more than *Summer Holi-*

*day*, which still draws great crowds when it is shown again.

His third musical film, *Wonderful Life*, also rang the till at the box office, but Cliff calls it a 'real disappointment.'

'We enjoyed the first two or three weeks' filming,' he recalls, 'but then it was obvious there were ructions in the camp, money problems and so on. The shooting got four weeks behind schedule, everybody got edgy, and it showed in our work. Sometimes we'd not start working until eleven a.m. because our temperamental director had kept us standing around while he gave us a monologue about how he was the captain of a sinking ship.'

In addition to these problems, the weather was awful. It had been planned that most of the film should be shot in the open, but, because of the weather, the entire story had to be changed and the thing was finally completed in the studio.

Yet the finished product, for all that, was a witty, sophisticated and entertaining film. Cliff played the part of a stunt man, which involved him in more than sixty costume changes. In one production number, 'History of the Movies'—'the best thing I've ever done on the screen'—he appeared in twenty different disguises and managed some very skilful impersonations.

The director of the film, Sid Furie, said this of his performance: 'Cliff is now the complete professional. He has an instinctive way of getting things done the right way. He has shown his talents as a dancer before, but in this production he has some really intricate dance steps and routines to handle. Gillian Lynne worked them all out and even she is surprised how Cliff managed to cope.'

In an interview in the *Daily Mirror*, Furie tried to answer the question, 'What puts Cliff at the top of Britain's box office stars?'

'He's a kind of Junior Cary Grant,' he replied. 'Not only girls want to mother him, mothers want to mother him. As far as his film career goes, he's only just beginning. I see him as a future international star, way up in the Rock Hudson class.'

In the same article Cliff's co-star in *Wonderful Life*, Susan Hampshire, denied any urge to mother him, but said, 'He knows every trick in the business. He can rave but he can also put over the tender thing, and when he does he makes you feel he is going to take care of you.'

His most recent film, *Finders Keepers*, is another musical comedy in the tradition of *Summer Holiday*. It does not have quite such memorable music, but it is several degrees funnier. Here Cliff and the Shadows appear as the complete professionals, acting with confidence and good technique and putting over the musical numbers expertly.

The story is loosely based on a real life incident in 1965, when the Americans lost an H-bomb in the sea off the coast of Spain.

'I wouldn't want anybody to get the idea that we

think H-bombs are funny,' Cliff comments, 'but our story is so farcical it couldn't possibly be considered to be in bad taste.'

Comedy stars Peggy Mount, Robert Morley and Graham Stark do much to enrich a not very inventive comic script, and Cliff and the Shadows exercise the old magnetism every time they pick up their guitars and sing.

With six films behind him, Cliff could reckon that his screen reputation was made, though he has a lingering ambition to make a non-musical film which would demand more from him as an actor. But, in a sense, films are artistically artificial. The whole thing depends so much on the director: people with very little acting ability, cleverly cast and directed, and allowing for hundreds of re-takes and dubbing, can be made to appear expert actors.

The live stage is still the real test of a performer, and it is here that Cliff has proved his qualities as an entertainer. The Palladium *Stars in Your Eyes* show and his Blackpool summer seasons in spectaculars demanded far more than a statuesque group of guitarists and a wriggling, gyrating soloist with a hand mike. Split second timing, confidence in handling a script, comic 'business' and dancing with a chorus were required. Cliff proved a ready learner, and coped happily with each successive demand on his talents.

The two big pantomimes at the London Palladium made further demands. *Aladdin* and *Cinderella* were virtually musical-comedy-spectaculars. No pantomimes in history had cost so much to stage, nor earned so much at the box office.

In both Cliff proved his personal magnetism and ability to create an instant *rapport* with the audience. Obviously enjoying it all hugely himself, he did not find it hard to communicate his enjoyment to the audience, from small children to grandparents. Both pantomimes were very happy shows, bringing immense pleasure to admittedly uncritical audiences, and *Cinderella* especially had some delightful new songs and dance numbers in it.

As Cliff became less and less bothered about his career and professional reputation, so he seemed to become more and more relaxed and happy on stage. His fans noticed the difference—'I began to realise he had something special,' one admirer of many years' standing noted, 'he had *real* joy and happiness, always a smile on his face.'

The explanation of Cliff's serenity was not that life at the top had suddenly become easier, but that he had now got it into proportion. Just as Cliff the rock 'n roller had grown up into Cliff Richard the polished entertainer, so Cliff the single-minded climber to the top had undergone a radical transformation of character.

It was not until 1966 that his admirers, who had noted the first change, had the second (and deeper) one dramatically brought to their attention.

## CHAPTER IX

## NEW SINGER, NEW SONG

TWENTY-FIVE thousand pairs of eyes followed the slim boyish figure as he walked up the steps to the rostrum. Wearing a brown corduroy jacket and dark-rimmed glasses, he had not looked out of place among the clergymen and other dignitaries on the platform as he had waited his turn to speak. Now it had come. Quietly, so that the public address system could barely pick it up, and many people in the vast audience had to lean forwards or crane their necks to hear, he began to tell them of his new-found faith as a Christian.

'I have never had the opportunity to speak to an audience as big as this before,' he began, 'but it is a great privilege to be able to tell so many people that I am a Christian . . .

'I can only say to people who are not Christians that until you have taken the step of asking Christ into your life, your life is not really worth while. It *works* —it works for me!'

The occasion was an evangelistic rally in the course of Billy-Graham's Greater London Crusade in June 1966. The speaker was Cliff Richard.

When he had said his piece, he sang a gospel song

('It's No Secret What God Can do')—'my voice is small,' he commented, 'but the message is a big one.'

After that, Cliff went outside with Billy Graham to say a few words to the five thousand people—mostly his own fans, it seemed—who had not been able to get into the Earls Court Stadium.

'Young people today ask if Christianity is relevant to them,' he told them, 'I can say most definitely that it is.'

Cliff's appearance at the Crusade (or 'his decision to join the Billy Graham set,' as the *Daily Mirror* put it) caused a major sensation. Every paper the next morning carried the story, most of them with pictures, and astonishment swept through the pop music world.

'He's not the type to take up religion,' wailed a teenage fan in *Disc*. 'He will lose a lot of fans,' declared another.

'I feel it is my duty,' was Cliff's comment, 'and the duty of all Christians, to tell as many people as possible about this wonderful thing I have discovered. Although I enjoy singing and making films, I have been searching for something deeper. Now I have discovered Christ. I want to help the cause of Christianity, but I am trying very hard not to give the impression of exploiting it by using my name.'

At the time, Cliff was filming *Finders Keepers* at Pinewood, and the set was suddenly swarming with reporters who wanted to know if he was giving up show business, if he was going to become a clergyman, if he was taking up preaching.

Cliff explained to them how he had come to appear on the world-famous evangelist's platform. He had been attending a six weeks' 'Christian Life and Witness' course, in company with over 20,000 other people from churches in the London area, in preparation for the Crusade. A tentative approach was made to him by the organisers—would he be willing to put in an appearance at one of the youth nights, say a few words, and sing?

'It took me quite a long time,' Cliff told the reporters, ' to pluck up enough courage to tell the world "I'm a Christian".'

But he accepted the invitation, and the result was the dramatic scene on the evening of Thursday June 16th. The *Daily Mirror* had somehow got wind of his appearance and carried an interview with Cliff on the subject in that morning's edition. The result was a mass turn-out of fans and others curious to see what Britain's top pop singer was doing at a religious rally.

'I was petrified,' Cliff confessed to the *New Musical Express* later. 'There was a desk in front of me, and I put my arms on it as I spoke. Then when I sang I put my arms to my side and had terrible pins and needles. I tried to raise my arms to emphasise words in the song, but I couldn't. And at the end I walked off with my arms still pinned to my side. Someone suggested' (it was the *Mirror*) 'that it is sissy to proclaim your Christian beliefs. I don't think it is.'

Actually Cliff must have been more scared than he

knew, because photos taken at the time show him raising his hands in natural gestures, but he has no recollection of it at all!

How did it come about that the star whose career
we have been tracing should end up on a Billy
Graham platform witnessing to his faith in Jesus
Christ? Religion has not played much part in the story
of his rise to the top of the show business ladder, yet
today Cliff would unhesitatingly say that Christianity
is far more important to him than his entertainment
career. That, coming from one of show business's
most dedicated and ambitious young men, represents
a very full circle indeed. Cliff's appearance at Earls
Court, and later persistent rumours of his impending
retirement from show business to become a teacher of
religious knowledge, took Fleet Street by surprise. But
it should not have done. Over the previous eighteen
months there had appeared revealing hints in inter
views and articles by his close associates of a changing
attitude on Cliff's part to life, work and the future.
The record papers, especially, had begun to sense that
something was going on in his mind which represented a deep change of heart.

As we have seen earlier, the Webbs' home in
Cheshunt was not without religious influence, and
Cliff would testify that those family Bible-reading
sessions made a lasting impression on him. Like many
children, he was taught to pray every night, and was
in a church choir in India.

Back in England, he and his mother used to go to church quite regularly for a period, but when his mother was working six evenings a week in a factory, Sunday became the only real family day. Strangely, although his father read the Bible to them, and clearly had a genuine faith of sorts, he would not attend church.

The reason he gave is an instructive one: 'Church is not for people like me.' He would maintain this with quiet insistence even to the local vicar, who used to visit the Webb home from time to time. This deep-rooted feeling that 'the Church' is not for ordinary working men, but rather belongs to some middle-class pressure-group, is a terrible indictment of the Church's failure in modern Britain to get over her message and meaning. If men like Mr. Webb, who pray and read their Bibles, feel the Church is 'not for them', then something is seriously wrong somewhere.

Be that as it may, the sort of religion found in the Webb household is certainly more widespread than most commentators of the religious scene would admit. It led quite logically to the sort of views Cliff expressed in the book *It's Great to be Young* written in 1960:

'There is one thing I feel very strongly about—religion. One's own religion. Whatever else becomes public, one's own beliefs should be private.'

That is the authentic voice of English religion, but, of course, if St. Paul and St. Augustine had kept their own beliefs private, we might still be running around in woad worshipping the sun! The idea that religion is a private line between individuals and God is one of the less helpful aspects of the British tradition of Protestant individualism.

Not only that, but popular religion requires vague, undogmatic beliefs:

'It's hard to explain but I believe in something; perhaps because we weren't actually there when Christ was on earth, it's hard to understand it. But I know there is something and it is that which makes everything worth while.

'But I don't believe in creeds and sects and that one person's religion is wrong because it isn't one's own. If you don't believe in anything, then what is there in life to hold on to? . . . It's so important to have faith in something, and it's equally important that no one ever laughs at you for the beliefs that you hold . . .

'I don't care if a person is Church of England, Jewish or Buddhist as long as he believes in something and is a decent person.'

It is easy for those of us with convinced Christian views to sneer at these sorts of sentiments. In fact, one must give Cliff—nineteen years old at the time, and enjoying the heady wine of success—full marks even for raising the subject and also for his obvious sincerity.

What he was saying is basically true: that there is an unknown factor in life ('something', he calls it no less than four times) which makes the whole confusing process worth while. He is too honest to give the 'something' a name (like luck, or Fate, or God). Like some Greek gentlemen described in the New Testament,[1] he is content to worship at the altar of an 'Unknown God'. But there is great virtue merely in knowing that this vital factor exists. 'So far as I can remember,' Cliff says now, 'I have never *not* believed in God, but until recently I did not really know who He is.'

Now many people are conscious of a missing factor in life, but never think that the explanation of it might lie with God. Cliff, perhaps because of his family background, naturally associated the two from the start, but seemed content to reduce God to a 'something' in which we should 'have faith'.

One reason for this may well be his comparative ignorance (in common with most of his fellow countrymen) of the contents of the Bible. Like most schoolboys, he decided that religion was strictly for girls and old ladies, and from about the age of fifteen did not open a Bible for six years or so.

He was busy, of course, carving out that path to the top that he pursued with such remarkable single-mindedness. 'My showbiz career took first place . . . I lived for it: I admit it.' Sundays were the best days for one-night stands; week-days were full of rehearsals, recording sessions, television shows and planning sessions. 'For three or four years we ate, drank and slept pop. We knew to get to the top you had to be

[1] Acts 17: 23.

dedicated, committed. We were going to the top, so . . .'

Cliff continued to pray from time to time, but on his own confession they were 'selfish' prayers: even they had to become part of the overriding commitment to success. One of the pop papers has a mildly embarrassing account of how Cliff once 'prayed' his third consecutive hit to the top of the charts.

The first hint of change came with his father's death in May 1961. For some months Mr. Webb had had poor health, and had already had one spell in hospital with heart trouble.

When Mrs. Webb and Cliff were called to the hospital on a Sunday evening they knew it could only be because his condition had suddenly deteriorated. He was in an oxygen tent, desperately ill, and obviously the end was near. When he died on the Monday morning it was the most painful blow Cliff had ever experienced.

'It was an absolutely shattering thing,' he recalls. 'One never really thinks it's going to happen. You must spend your whole life realising people *do* die, but when it happens to someone very near you it's a terrific blow.'

For some time, of course, Mrs. Webb, Cliff and the girls had given mental assent to the idea that Dad was a sick man and could die quite suddenly. But he had seemed to improve over the previous two or three months, and the darker ideas had been pushed away from the front of their minds. And then; in the space of just a few days, he had collapsed, was rushed to hospital, and died.

The Webbs, as we have seen, were a very closely knit family, and Cliff had enjoyed a very deep and happy relationship with his father. Since 1960 Mr. Webb had not had an ordinary job, but had helped Cliff professionally in a hundred practical ways and had entered fully into the business and planning side of his career. Cliff was used to trying out new ideas on his father and discussing plans and projects with him. Now all that was ended.

As the eldest son, Cliff had a number of responsibilities, especially towards his mother; and carrying these out softened the blow a little. But when a human relationship of such intimacy is broken, the scars remain for a long time.

Some months later, when Cliff and the Shadows were touring in Australia, one quite unexpected effect of his father's death began to make itself felt. Cliff had a growing desire to 'get in touch' with Dad. He had never been at all superstitious, and is in fact a fairly down-to-earth sort of person, but he could not rid his mind of this notion.

Always in the past he had talked things over with his father, got his advice, accepted his guidance. If the spiritualists were right—and who could say they were not?—then there was no reason why his father's death should stop that happening. Perhaps it was being in a

distant land, and homesick; or perhaps it was the pain-
fully growing awareness that comes to the bereaved
some time after the event, that the loved one is gone
beyond recall : whatever it was, Cliff felt it acutely.

'I just reckoned that if there was some way of getting in touch with him I'd try it. If these people were
spiritual, then what was the harm in using them to ask
Dad a few questions about what was going to happen
and so on?'

So Cliff planned to go to a spiritualist seance. But
he was not entirely easy about it. He is one of those
people who like to analyse a decision before taking it,
and then stick to it whatever happens. In the course of
this analysis he asked for Brian Locking's opinion.
Brian (currently the Shadows' bass guitarist) thought
for a moment.

'Do you really want my opinion?' he asked.

'Sure.'

'Then I'm dead against it.'

'Why?'

'Have you ever studied what the Bible has to say
about it?'

Cliff had not been asked a question like that for
years. It had not seriously occurred to him even to
take into account what the Bible might, or might not,
say about it.

Brian showed him a number of passages in the Bible
where God warned of the dire dangers of consulting
mediums.[1] Cliff was surprised to find that one of his

[1] Leviticus 20 : 27; Isaiah 8 : 19.

closest colleagues took the Bible so seriously and knew his way around it so well. It made him feel that he, too, ought to know rather more about the contents of this book.

Discussion on the topic of spiritualism led on into discussion of many other subjects in the light of the Bible. Brian Locking was a devoted Jehovah's Witness, and, like most members of the sect, was very knowledgeable about several little-read parts of the Bible, including books like Daniel and Revelation. Soon informal Bible studies, involving Cliff and three of the Shadows and—when they got back to Britain in November 1961—some of Brian's Jehovah's Witness friends, became a regular feature of their tours together.

Cliff also began reading the Bible on his own. At first he tried the Authorised (King James) version, but found 350-year-old English rather heavy going. He asked Brian's advice, and was given a copy of the Jehovah's Witness translation, *The New World Bible*. Whatever its merits or demerits as a translation, this is at least in twentieth century English, and Cliff used to read a chapter or so a day.

Slowly his scale of values began to change. 'It suddenly hit me,' he says, 'that there was more to life than I thought there was—that the things I had weren't satisfying.' He had begun a slow pilgrimage to faith.

This period—1962–3—was a very busy one for them. Overseas tours, a long Palladium season, summer shows at Blackpool, television series and a steady stream of records kept Cliff and the Shadows very busy. With more leisure, Cliff's pursuit of the truth might have produced more immediate results. As it was, he continued to read his Bible, ask questions and probe the truth.

He found the beliefs of the Jehovah's Witnesses interesting and logical. They seemed to have an answer to every question, and to get those answers from the Bible. Their religion made sense, it provided purpose and motive for life, and it clearly meant a great deal to them. Cliff has always respected dedication and commitment in others, and these were the first people he had met who were totally dedicated and committed to a religion and to God. He also had an aunt whom he much respected who was a Jehovah's Witness. Perhaps here was the answer to the problem of the 'unknown factor' in life?

Cliff began attending the Witnesses' meetings at their 'Kingdom Halls' up and down the country. Indeed, during a summer season at Blackpool in this period he used to attend the meeting every Sunday afternoon. He was never in one place long enough to get to know many Witnesses personally—other than Brian and his aunt, of course—but he gained quite a grasp of their doctrines.

Jehovah's Witnesses are followers of a movement begun by a man called Russell in the nineteenth century. Their most distinctive beliefs are that the Trinity (the orthodox Christian doctrine that there

are three Persons in the Godhead, Father, Son and
Holy Spirit) is a false notion: Jehovah (God) is a
single deity, and Jesus Christ is a created being like—
though superior to—the angels. The Holy Spirit is
simply the breath of 'influence' of God in the world.
They also believe that Jesus Christ returned, though
secretly, in 1915; that soon God's reign on earth will
come, with the Witnesses as rulers of the nations; and
that only a few—the 'Jonadabs'—will actually attain
to Heaven: 144,000 of them to be precise.

Summarised like that, their views may sound a little
odd. But, given their own interpretation of certain
parts of scripture, the whole thing does form quite a
consistent and logical pattern, with a particular appeal
for the sort of person who likes his religion strong and
neat.

During this stage of events Cliff and Hank (especially) came strongly under the influence of the sect's
teachings. Both of them stopped swearing, and religious debates and discussions raged interminably.
Cliff was almost, but not entirely, persuaded.

Once a Roman Catholic priest came up to him—at
Blackpool—to tackle him on the subject of 'this
Jehovah's Witness heresy.' Cliff was quite interested
to meet somebody 'from the other side', and put a
number of very penetrating questions to him on the
subject of the Trinity. Unfortunately the priest merely
insisted that it was 'all a divine mystery', and retired
muttering that 'you've obviously read more than I
thought you had.'

Cliff's mother and sisters had also got interested in the Witnesses, especially Jackie, who eventually was baptised into the sect and now works full-time for the movement.

One of the things that impressed Cliff about the Witnesses was that wherever you went, anywhere in Britain and all over the world, you could find these little congregations, and everywhere you would hear exactly the same teachings. There was an incredible *unity* about the movement.

'After a while,' Cliff recalls, 'I began to feel like a Jehovah's Witness myself, but for some reason I held back from being baptised. If I hadn't been in showbiz, who knows, I might have done; but I just didn't feel I wanted to be quite so committed to it yet.'

This period of Jehovah's Witness influence was a long one, covering most of 1962 up to almost the end of 1964. During it Cliff became more serious and all the while he was reading the Bible and asking questions.

Then came an apparently chance conversation with an old friend, and once again the direction of Cliff's life was drastically altered.

He had always gone back regularly to see his old English teacher, Mrs. Norris. She, alone of his friends of pre-pop days, still insisted on calling him Harry. He even went back to school and took a class for her once.

Although Jay Norris was a Roman Catholic, they had never, so far as Cliff could recollect, discussed religion. But on one occasion in 1964, when he paid

her one of his periodical visits, the conversation got on
to the subject of religion. Cliff treated her to a full
length exposition of his views, which were, of course,
a pretty well undiluted version of the Jehovah's Witnesses' beliefs.

Jay Norris listened to them patiently. Sensing that
Cliff was himself not as convinced as he sounded, and
that he was really inviting her comments on his views,
she said, 'I don't have the answers, Harry. But I know
someone who has. There's a young R.I. teacher at
school . . . he's the very person you should talk to.'

Cliff agreed to meet the person in question, and a
date was fixed when Jay Norris would bring him to
Rookswood.

When the time came, three people in fact turned up
at Cliff's palatial residence: Jay Norris, the R.I.
teacher from Cheshunt, Bill Latham and Bill's friend
Graham Disbrey, who was also a schoolteacher.

The subject for the evening was already decided so,
almost without preliminaries, the discussion began.
'We thrashed and thrashed over things for hours and
hours,' Cliff recalls. He did not feel that they really
answered all his questions by any means, but he found
the people more compelling than their views.

Bill and Graham were just ordinary, 'orthodox'
Christians—Bill is an Anglican, Graham a Baptist.
They believed passionately that the Bible is God's
inspired guide for life and truth, and that a personal
trust in Jesus Christ as a man's Saviour and Master is
the only way to forgiveness and eternal life.

Bill and Graham may not have been great saints, but they were transparently sincere and totally committed Christians. Once again, Cliff responded to dedication in others. 'They were the first real Christians I had met, talking about the real thing, appealing only to the Bible, but interested in me as a *person*, not a scalp.' Although Cliff was at loggerheads with them all the evening, and did not feel that they had seriously upset his Jehovah's Witness views, yet he was more impressed than he cared to admit.

Again, it might have ended there, but Jay Norris invited Cliff to a party and there he met Bill again. This time they did not argue about religious doctrine. Instead Cliff quizzed Bill about his own life, about his main leisure-time activity as a leader of a local branch of a Christian youth movement, the Crusaders. In that unaffected way in which dedicated people talk about their main interests in life (and Cliff knew all about *that*) Bill told him of the outings and camps, the Broads cruises and the Sunday Bible classes; and also of his own personal commitment to Jesus Christ.

Bill invited him to come along to some of the Crusader activities, and so the Finchley Crusader class —some sixty boys between the ages of eight and eighteen—had the unexpected privilege of a personal visit from Britain's top singer.

But it was not as a 'top singer' that Cliff went there. He went because of that unknown factor, the missing ingredient that makes everything worth while. He went because he wanted to know why another young

man of his own age should give his spare time to helping young boys grow up with a solid foundation in life and a living faith. He came because this was about as far from the echoing, empty world of stardom as he could get. He sat at the back, and watched and listened. 'Slowly,' he recalled, 'it began to mean something to me.'

First of all it meant something in terms of friendship. 'I had many acquaintances in the showbiz world, and a few people I admired. But beyond the Shadows and my manager it would be hard to say I had any friends. My old friends from school days seemed awestruck and were awkward with me. New "friends" cropped up. They filled my flat when I was in town, and drank my drinks, but there was no reality about it.

'Now, at last, these people were offering me friendship as a person, not as a star.'

He realised that he was something of a 'catch' for any movement or church. 'I've always been able to tell pretty well when people are genuine. I was quite sure that Bill, Graham and the other Christians I met were completely sincere . . . I felt they were *real* people.'

His admiration for the Christians he got to know, however, did not automatically change his views. For a long while he would not go to church with them, for instance. Further long debates on the Bible and Christian doctrine followed, mostly centring on the question of the divinity of Jesus Christ, and the Trinity. Nobody was going to fob Cliff off with easy answers.

He was still reading the Bible regularly—only now he was using the New English Bible version—and he ruthlessly tested all he was told against what he read.

But the thing that was slowly forming in his mind was the root of it all: that the Christian gospel is not primarily a set of doctrines or propositions, but a matter of trusting a living person, God's Son, Jesus Christ. One night, after a lengthy discussion involving half a dozen people, Cliff summed it all up.

'If I want to be a real Christian, exactly what do I have to do?'

'Admit and confess your sin,' came the reply, 'believe that Jesus Christ died so that you could be forgiven, and put your whole trust in Him.'

The gathering slowly broke up in a fairly serious mood. As people were leaving, Cliff said quietly to Bill, 'I'm on my way in.' He certainly was. And one sign of it was that from then on he has been a regular church-goer.

'I had thought myself a Christian before,' he recalls, 'but discovered I was not. Jesus Christ is a living Saviour, and to be a Christian is to *know* Him, to accept the fact that He died for us. That is what happened to me.'

It was at about this time—the summer of 1965— that hints began to drop from Cliff's lips in public quarters that show business was no longer the be-all and end-all of life for him.

'I've been in this game so long now. I've achieved most of the things I've set myself to do . . . Now I must find something else to aim at,' he said in an interview in a women's magazine.

'Pop life can't go on forever,' he told a *Disc Weekly* reporter. 'I wouldn't miss much of this life . . . You see, I want to do something worthwhile with my life.'

In private he was even more explicit. 'I've wanted to teach for some time,' he once told me, 'and now that I've seen what an influence a Christian teacher can have on the kids I'm really keen to do it.' This has become a growing conviction—that, provided he can pass the exams, his future lies in the classroom rather than on the stage. When he leaves show business, though, it will be from the top. He has no intention of slowly fading out.

During the autumn of 1965 Cliff's commitment as a practising Christian became absolute. This showed itself in many ways. On the public level, he began to talk quite freely about his faith, and the Christian activities in which he was increasingly involved. He made no secret of his convictions where his immediate colleagues and show-business friends were concerned.

At the private level, his own life changed decisively. His old interests and priorities were, in many cases, turned upside down. Prayer—once an occasional, selfish exercise—became (in his own words) 'direct communication with God.' His time was increasingly spent either with Christian friends or in the activities of the Crusaders—he was appointed an assistant leader in December 1965—and his own local church.

The boys in the Crusaders had learnt to accept him

long before. Back in the Easter of 1965 Bill had invited him to join them on a Broads cruise—a holiday in motor cruisers for boys from a number of local classes. Cliff had wondered whether to accept. Would it be a drag? How could he possibly come to terms with several boatloads of scruffy schoolboys? But he accepted, feeling that if it meant so much to Bill and the others, there must be some good in it. There was just a tinge of awkwardness on the first evening as the boys met the famous Cliff, but before bed-time that was gone—dispelled for ever when two young horrors ambushed him and flung him to the ground. This was routine treatment for leaders . . . but for Mr. Richard? He rose from the ground grinning, the boys relaxed, and from then on he was just 'Cliff', fully accepted as himself.

The youth fellowship at  St. Paul's (Anglican) church was a bit more of a problem, mainly because it was mixed. At first some of the girls tended to sit and goggle, but as they realised that Cliff was in every way completely normal and as he carefully treated everybody, boys or girls, in exactly the same open, sensible way, the shyness melted and again he was completely accepted and liked as a person.

Cliff appreciated this deeply. 'After all,' he points out, 'the fans don't think of you as a person, and even ordinary people who meet you always seem to want your autograph if you're well known on TV or the films. Now, as soon as somebody asks for your autograph, an ordinary social relationship between you becomes difficult, for they have immediately put you on a sort of pedestal. True, some of the people at church and Crusaders have asked for autographs, but they *haven't* put me on a pedestal!'

Some of his show business friends found all this rather hard to accept. For one thing, they could not possibly imagine what pleasure Cliff would derive from the company of people not connected with the entertainment world.

'Showbiz is the most "in" world of all,' Cliff explains, 'Almost the sole topic of conversation is one's fellow performers: who's up, who's down, who's in, who's out. They think that to spend an evening with people who don't share that interest would be an awful drag.'

In fact, show business company was beginning to be a bit of a drag for Cliff. He had never been very keen on it, preferring to go home after a show rather than spend night after night in town. 'If there's nothing to do in town, why not go home?' had always been Cliff's line, but most of the show business set hang around the West End all the time.

Now Cliff slipped away whenever he could, to share in Crusader outings to the zoo or for football, or just to spend a pleasant evening with his fellow-Christians. Cliff's guitar was often fetched out to accompany some of the catchy gospel songs that were going the rounds.

At a special youth service in his church Cliff played and sang a simple gospel song to the tune of 'Blowin' in the Wind'. He did it anonymously, and few of the older members of the congregation knew who he was.

It was much the same when he visited the local hospital at Christmas time. He played and sang in one of the wards, and an elderly patient remarked that he was quite good, really—'he ought to take it up.'

Still the rumours persisted in the pop music papers that Cliff was thinking of retiring. He made no secret, now, of the fact that he helped with a Christian youth movement and went to church regularly; nor did he deny that he was beginning to look beyond the end of his show business career, whenever that might come.

Despite all this the national papers were taken by surprise when Cliff appeared on Billy Graham's platform to tell the world that he was a Christian, with the life of Jesus Christ in his heart. That evening—'definitely the most tremendous moment of my whole life'—was the point of no return for 'Christian Cliff', as *Disc* had taken to calling him. He knew that from now on his every public action and remark would be judged as the action or remark of a Christian.

In fact, Cliff had been to the Earls Court Crusade meetings several times before. Declining to seek celebrity treatment (which he could have had, needless to say, for the asking) he went with the youth fellowship from his church, and sat with them, enjoying for once the anonymity of a face in a crowd of over twenty thousand.

Cliff was very impressed with Billy Graham. He has always approved of preachers with some body in their sermons, and he appreciated Graham's constant appeal to the Bible as his authority. Not only that: Cliff knows something about being a celebrity and having the adulation of the crowds. He had the opportunity to see at close hand how Graham's openness and frankness remained unspoiled, and how he constantly tried to direct his hearers' attention away from himself and up to God.

'I know people criticise the Billy Graham kind of conversion,' he argues, 'but if it doesn't last, then it wasn't real in the first place. People who were moved by what I said that night at Earls Court might look back in a couple of years' time and think it was a whole load of rubbish ... Either you take it, or you don't; no holds barred!'

Earls Court was not Cliff's first public appearance at a big religious meeting, but it was the first one the Press learned about. Some months before, in April, he had been interviewed on the stage of the Central Hall, Westminster, before a capacity audience of two thousand seven hundred teen-agers at an Anglican youth rally, and he had sung and played his guitar at a Crusader rally in the same building some time before that.

Later, in the autumn of 1966, Cliff undertook a number of engagements of this sort, singing gospel songs and giving a few words of 'testimony'. Hundreds of his fans were shut out of the famous Empire Theatre, Liverpool, when he appeared at an Eric Hutchings Crusade meeting there; and a crowd of five thousand heard him sing in the Royal Albert Hall at a service to mark the twenty-fifth anniversary of the Lee Abbey Christian community, at the invitation of the Bishop of Coventry.

But it would be misleading to imply that the main effect of Cliff's conversion has been to boost the numbers at religious meetings. Its most important effect has been upon him, which is as it should be. Such public appearances at Christian meetings and rallies are very strictly rationed, but the day-in and day-out Christian life goes on.

How has being a committed Christian affected his approach to show business?

'It has put it in perspective,' Cliff says. 'I used to live for beat and to see my records in the charts. I used to be jealous of artists whose records did better than mine—and believe me, there's plenty of jealousy in showbiz. Now I think I can get my priorities right . . . I can enjoy success or popularity without being obsessed by them.

'Now I see entertaining people as my job, at least for the present. I know it's not the most important thing in the world, but I must do it as well as I can. The people who come have paid to see a good show, and it's my duty to entertain them as well as I can, or get out of show business.

'The funny thing is, that since I've become a Christian I am more relaxed and happy on stage, and I think if anything my work has improved a bit—in terms of entertainment.

'When I say I am a Christian, that means I must be

a Christian all the time. Not just on stage, or off stage, but in everything I do.

'I know I am a happier and more balanced person, and I am more careful than ever about the sort of words I sing, and things like that. The whole quality of life has improved, that is the difference ... I feel really great!'

It is absolutely typical of Cliff that having set himself to something, he should give it everything. Nominal Christianity has no appeal for him, it must be the real thing, or nothing.

This has made him an excellent advocate for Christianity. In Crusaders, where he takes his turn at giving a Bible talk every few weeks, he is a popular speaker. He talks very quickly (as usual), but with that liveliness and enthusiasm that light up all he touches. In personal conversation with people, especially in the showbiz world, he is well able to give a good account of himself in any discussion about religion.

During the time of the Billy Graham Crusade he went out of his way to invite his hard core of fans, who follow him everywhere, to the meetings. He even got tickets for some of them, and stood explaining the gospel to one of them for nearly an hour after the meeting one night. The result was that a number of them were converted—and time has proved that this, at least, was not just a case of 'following Cliff wherever he goes.'

His latest venture in Christian witness may well prove to be the most effective of all. The feature film in which he is starring, to be shot in the summer of 1967 in England by the Billy Graham-owned World Wide Pictures company, may well prove to be the first evangelistic film made in Britain to achieve a really nation-wide impact. Director Jim Collier is a gifted and creative man, and he is convinced that Cliff, playing the role of a cynical, self-seeking materialist who has his illusions shattered by events, is going to produce the finest performance of his career.

Whether he does or not, this film may well mark yet another field of endeavour to be entered and mastered by Cliff Richard. But more important to him, this time, will be the underlying purpose of the film—to probe the realities of life, and throw light on that 'unknown factor' which 'makes everything worth while.'

For this was the very thing Cliff had discovered for himself. It was not that the world of showbiz disgusted him, or that he had got bored with success. It was simply that it had come to lack meaning or purpose. The dominant question was not 'What's it worth?' so much as 'What's it for?'

The great drive to the top had consumed all Cliff's thinking and purpose since adolescence. Once he had got there, life was temporarily deprived of purpose or ambition. Until one reaches the top rung of the ladder, one can always hope that the next step up will bring complete fulfilment. But once one has reached the top, and still not found that fulfilment, then a different search must begin. The depression and despair of many people in the top levels of show business is well enough known—no group of people has a higher suicide rate. These are the ones, it seems, who have found that total success does not equal total fulfilment, and having reached the end of their ambitions have no idea where else to look for it.

Cliff certainly found total success. The whole world of show business lay at his feet. He had more money than he could spend. Every whim could be indulged. He was not morose, or depressed, or desperate, by any means. Yet he knew that there was something missing, and the search for that something brought him to God. Here, in the One who made him, and in following Jesus Christ, was purpose and fulfilment. Life for the genuine Christian has direction, meaning and destination; or, in the simpler but more telling words of Christ Himself, way, truth and life.[1] Cliff had always found—as most people do—that it is in living relationships (with family or friends) that most satisfaction is to be found, rather than in philosophies of life. What more natural, then, that real fulfilment should be discovered, not in a philosophy or theory, but in living relationship with Jesus Christ.

Those who know him best are quite unanimous that Cliff now is a happier and more serene person than the Cliff of three years ago. 'Cliff is the happiest person I have ever met,' said the girl who played opposite him in the film *Finders Keepers*, Vivienne Ventura. 'He is older, wiser, more mature,' wrote a film corre-

[1] John 14:6—see also John 1:12, 10:10.

spondent. His closest friends have noted the change in him, too—probably more than Cliff has himself.

Although Cliff had been baptised as a baby, he had never been confirmed. Now he felt drawn to make this formal and public commitment to Jesus Christ and the Church. Along with a handful of other adults he went through the usual course of instruction over a period of several months, and finally, on December 6th, 1966, in his own church, he was confirmed by the Bishop of Willesden.

It was an occasion to remember for Cliff and his friends, the church filled with the relatives and friends of the candidates and the centuries-old rite, filled with meaning for those who take it seriously, providing a simple opportunity for them to accept as mature people all the implications of Christian commitment.

Two by two the candidates filed out to kneel before the bishop, who laid his hands on their heads and prayed that God would strengthen them with the Holy Spirit to live the Christian life. Many people in the church knew already that Cliff was a candidate, or recognised him as he sat, slightly nervous as ever, next to the young solicitor's clerk who had gone through the same course of instruction with him, waiting for their turn to go forward.

'Defend, O Lord, this thy child *Cliff* . . .' the bishop prayed. People around the church half smiled in recognition of the name. It was another moment of truth in Cliff's life, made all the happier by the fact that his mother was there ('I wouldn't have missed it, anyway,' she said afterwards), although Cliff's religion had taken a rather different course from that of the rest of the family.

It was another great turning point, in its way: like Hoddesdon, and Butlin's, and *Oh Boy!* and Earls Court; and yet so natural, so easy, that it seemed that all his life up to this moment had merely been a preparation for it. It was—and no simile could possibly please Cliff more—just like coming home.

# APPENDIX

## CLIFF RICHARD'S CAREER IN FACTS AND FIGURES

### A. RECORDS

| SINGLES | RELEASED |
|---|---|
| Move It/Schoolboy Crush | *Aug. 1958* |
| High Class Baby/My Feet Hit The Ground | *Nov. 1958* |
| Livin' Lovin' Doll/Steady With You | *Jan. 1959* |
| Mean Streak/Never Mind | *Apr. 1959* |
| Living Doll/Apron Strings | *July 1959* |
| Travellin' Light/Dynamite | *Oct. 1959* |
| A Voice In The Wilderness/Don't Be Mad At Me | *Jan. 1960* |
| Fall In Love With You/Willie & The Hand Jive | *Mar. 1960* |
| Please Don't Tease/Where Is My Heart | *June 1960* |
| Nine Times Out Of Ten/Thinking Of Our Love | *Sept. 1960* |
| I Love You/'D' In Love | *Dec. 1960* |
| Theme For A Dream/Mumblin' Mosie | *Feb. 1961* |
| A Girl Like You/Now's The Time To Fall In Love | *June 1961* |
| When The Girl In Your Arms Is The Girl In Your Heart/Got a Funny Feeling | *Oct. 1961* |
| The Young Ones/We Say Yeah | *Jan. 1962* |
| I'm Lookin' Out The Window/Do You Want To Dance | *May 1962* |
| It'll Be Me/Since I Lost You | *Aug. 1962* |
| The Next Time/Bachelor Boy | *Nov. 1962* |
| Summer Holiday/Dancing Shoes | *Feb. 1963* |
| Lucky Lips/I Wonder | *May 1963* |
| It's All In The Game/Your Eyes Tell On You | *Aug. 1963* |
| Don't Talk To Him/Say You're Mine | *Nov. 1963* |
| I'm The Lonely One/Watch What You Do With My Baby | *Jan. 1964* |

| | |
|---|---|
| Constantly/True True Lovin' | *Apr. 1964* |
| On The Beach/A Matter Of Moments | *June 1964* |
| The Twelfth Of Never/I'm Afraid To Go Home | *Oct. 1964* |
| I Could Easily Fall In Love With You/I'm In Love With You | *Nov. 1964* |
| The Minute You're Gone/Just Another Guy | *Mar. 1965* |
| On My Word/Just A Little Bit Too Late | *June 1965* |
| Time In Between/Look Before You Love | *Aug. 1965* |
| Wind Me Up (Let Me Go)/The Night | *Oct. 1965* |
| Blue Turns To Grey/Somebody Loses | *Feb. 1966* |
| Visions/What Would I Do (For The Love Of A Girl) | *July 1966* |
| Time Drags By/La La La Song | *Oct. 1966* |
| In The Country/Finders Keepers | *Dec. 1966* |
| It's All Over/Why Wasn't I Born Rich | *Apr. 1967* |
| I'll Come Runnin'/I Get The Feelin' | *June 1967* |
| The Day I Met Marie/Our Story Book | *Sept. 1967* |
| All My Love/Sweet Little Jesus Boy | *Nov. 1967* |
| Congratulations/High and Dry (Eurovision Song Contest) | *Mar. 1968* |

E.P.'S                                    RELEASED

*Serious Charge*                          *May 1959*
Living Doll, No Turning Back, Mad About You. (The Shadows: Chinchilla).
*Cliff No. 1.*                            *June 1959*
Apron Strings, My Babe, Down The Line, I Gotta Feeling, Baby I Don't Care.
*Cliff No. 2.*                            *July 1959*
Donna, Move It, Ready Teddy, Too Much, Don't Bug Me Baby.
*Expresso Bongo*                          *Jan. 1960*
Love, A Voice In The Wilderness, The Shrine On The Second Floor. (The Shadows: Bongo Blues).
*Cliff Sings No. 1.*                      *Feb. 1960*
Here Comes Summer, I Gotta Know, Blue Suede Shoes, The Snake And The Bookworm.
*Cliff Sings No. 2.*                      *Mar. 1960*
Twenty Flight Rock, Pointed Toe Shoes, Mean Woman

Blues, I'm Walkin'.
*Cliff Sings No. 3.*                                    *1960*
I'll String Along With You, Embraceable You, As Time
Goes By, The Touch Of Your Lips.
*Cliff Sings No. 4.*                              *Sept. 1960*
I Don't Know Why (I Just Do), Little Things Mean A Lot,
Somewhere Along The Way, That's My Desire.
*Cliff's Silver Discs*                             *Dec. 1960*
Please Don't Tease, Fall In Love With You, Nine Times
Out Of Ten, Travellin' Light.
*Me And My Shadows No. 1.*                         *Feb. 1961*
I'm Gonna Get You, You And I, I Cannot Find A True
Love, Evergreen Tree, She's Gone.
*Me And My Shadows No. 2.*                         *Mar. 1961*
Left Out Again, You're Just The One To Do It, Lamp Of
Love, Choppin' 'n Changin', We Have It Made.
*Me And My Shadows No. 3.*                         *Apr. 1961*
Tell Me, Gee Whiz It's You, I'm Willing To Learn, I Love
You So, I Don't Know.
*Listen To Cliff No. 1.*                           *Oct. 1961*
What'd I Say, True Love Will Come To You, Blue Moon,
Lover.
*Dream*                                            *Nov. 1961*
Dream, All I Do Is Dream Of You, I'll See You In My
Dreams, When I Grow Too Old To Dream.
*Listen To Cliff No. 2.*                           *Dec. 1961*
Unchained Melody, First Lesson In Love, Idle Gossip,
Almost Like Being In Love, Beat Out Dat Rhythm On A
Drum.
*Cliff's Hit Parade*                               *Feb. 1962*
I Love You, Theme For A Dream, A Girl Like You, When
The Girl In Your Arms Is The Girl In Your Heart.
*Cliff Richard No. 1.*                             *Apr. 1962*
Forty Days, Catch Me, How Wonderful To Know, Tough
Enough.
*Hits From 'The Young Ones'*                       *May 1962*
The Young Ones, Got A Funny Feeling, Lessons In Love,
We Say Yeah.

*Cliff Richard No. 2.*                                      *June 1962*
50 Tears For Every Kiss, The Night Is So Lonely, Poor
Boy, Y'Arriva.

*Cliff's Hits*                                             *Nov. 1962*
It'll Be Me, Since I Lost You, Do You Want To Dance,
I'm Looking Out The Window.

*Time For Cliff And The Shadows*                           *Mar. 1963*
So I've Been Told, I'm Walkin' The Blues, When My
Dreamboat Comes Home, Blueberry Hill, You Don't
Know.

*Holiday Carnival*                                         *May 1963*
Carnival, Moonlight Bay, Some Of These Days, For You
For Me.

*Hits From 'Summer Holiday'*                               *June 1963*
Summer Holiday, The Next Time, Dancing Shoes, Bachelor
Boy.

*More Hits from 'Summer Holiday'*                          *Sept. 1963*
Seven Days To A Holiday, Stranger In Town, Really Waltzing, All At Once.

*Cliff's Lucky Lips*                                       *Oct. 1963*
It's All In The Game, Your Eyes Tell On You, Lucky Lips,
I Wonder.

*Love Songs*                                               *Nov. 1963*
I'm In The Mood For Love, Secret Love, Love Letters, I
Only Have Eyes For You.

*When In France*                                           *Feb. 1964*
La Mer, Boum, J'Attendrai, C'Est Si Bon.

*Cliff Sings Don't Talk To Him*                            *Mar. 1964*
Don't Talk To Him, Say You're Mine, Spanish Harlem,
Who Are We To Say, Falling In Love With Love.

*Cliff's Palladium Successes*                              *May 1964*
I'm The Lonely One, Watch What You Do With My Baby,
Perhaps Perhaps Perhaps, Frenesi.

*Wonderful Life*                                           *Aug. 1964*
Wonderful Life, Do You Remember, What've I Gotta Do,
Walkin'.

*A Forever Kind Of Love*                                   *Sept. 1964*
A Forever Kind Of Love, It's Wonderful To Be Young,
Constantly, True True Lovin'.

*Wonderful Life No. 2.*                        *Oct. 1964*
Matter Of Moments, Girl In Every Port, A Little Imagination, In the Stars.
*Hits From 'Wonderful Life'*                        *Dec. 1964*
On The Beach, We Love A Movie, Home, All Kinds Of People.
*Why Don't They Understand*                        *Feb. 1965*
Why Don't They Understand, Where The Four Winds Blow, The Twelfth of Never, I'm Afraid To Go Home.
*Cliff's Hits From 'Aladdin And His Wonderful Lamp'*
                                        *Mar. 1965*
Havin' Fun, Evening Comes, Friends, I Could Easily Fall (In Love With You).
*Look In My Eyes Maria*                        *May 1965*
Look In My Eyes Maria, Where Is Your Heart, Maria, If I Give My Heart To You.
*Angel*                                        *Sept. 1965*
Angel, I Only Came To Say Goodbye, On My Word, The Minute You're Gone.
*Take Four*                                *Oct. 1965*
Boom Boom, My Heart Is An Open Book, Lies & Kisses, Sweet & Gentle.
*Wind Me Up*                                *Feb. 1966*
Wind Me up, The Night, The Time In Between, Look Before You Love.
*Hits From When In Rome*                        *Apr. 1966*
Come Prima (For The First Time), Nel Blu Dipinto Di Blu (Volare), Dicitencello Vuie (Just Say I Love Her), Arriverderci Roma.
*Love Is Forever*                                *June 1966*
My Colouring Book, Fly Me To The Moon, Someday, Everyone Needs Someone To Love.
*La La La La La*                                *Dec. 1966*
La La La La La, Solitary Man, Things We Said Today, Never Knew What Love Could Do.
*Cinderella*                                *May 1967*
Come Sunday, Peace And Quiet, She Needs Him More Than Me, Hey Doctor Man.

*Carol Singers*                                        *Nov. 1967*
God Rest You Merry Gentlemen, In the Bleak Midwinter,
Unto Us a Boy Is Born, While Shepherds Watched, Little
Town of Bethlehem.


L.P.'S                                                RELEASED
*Cliff*                                                 *Apr. 1959*
Apron Strings, My Babe, Down The Line, I Got A Feeling,
Jet Black (The Drifters), Baby I Don't Care, Donna, Move
It, Ready Teddy, Too Much, Don't Bug Me Baby, Driftin'
(The Drifters), That'll Be The Day, Be-Bop-A-Lula (The
Drifters), Danny, Whole Lotta Shakin' Goin' On.
*Cliff Sings*                                           *Nov. 1959*
Blue Suede Shoes, The Snake And The Bookworm, I Gotta
Know, Here Comes Summer, I'll String Along With You,
Embraceable You, As Time Goes By, The Touch Of Your
Lips, Twenty Flight Rock, Pointed Toe Shoes, Mean
Woman Blues, I'm Walking, I Don't Know Why, Little
Things Mean A Lot, Somewhere Along The Way, That's
My Desire.
*Me And My Shadows*                                    *Oct. 1960*
I'm Gonna Get You, You And I, I Cannot Find A True
Love, Evergreen Tree, She's Gone, Left Out Again, You're
Just The One To Do It, Lamp Of Love, Choppin' 'n
Changin', We Have It Made, Tell Me, Gee Whiz It's You,
I Love You So, I'm Willing To Learn, I Don't Know,
Working After School.
*Listen to Cliff*                                       *May 1961*
What'd I Say, Blue Moon, Trust Love Will Come To You,
Lover, Unchained Melody, Idle Gossip, First Lesson In
Love, Almost Like Being In Love, Beat Out Dat Rhythm
On A Drum, Memories Linger On, Temptation, I Live For
You, Sentimental Journey, I Want You To Know, We
Kiss In A Shadow, It's You.
*21 Today*                                              *Oct. 1961*
Happy Birthday To You, Forty Days, Catch Me, How
Wonderful To Know, Tough Enough, 50 Tears For Every
Kiss, The Night Is So Lonely, Poor Boy, Y'Arriva, Out-
sider, Tea For Two, To Prove My Love For You, Without

You, A Mighty Lonely Man, My Blue Heaven, Shame On You.

*The Young Ones*                                    Dec. 1961

Friday Night, Got A Funny Feeling, Peace Pipe, Nothing's Impossible, The Young Ones, All For One, Lessons In Love, No One For Me But Nicky, What D'You Know We've Got A Show & Vaudeville Routine, When The Girl In Your Arms Is The Girl In Your Heart, Just Dance, Mood Mambo, The Savage, We Say Yeah.

*32 Minutes And 17 Seconds With Cliff Richard*  Oct. 1962

It'll Be Me, So I've Been Told, How Long Is Forever, I'm Walkin' The Blues, Turn Around, Blueberry Hill, Let's Make A Memory, When My Dreamboat Comes Home, I'm On My Way, Spanish Harlem, You Don't Know, Falling In Love With Love, Who Are We To Say, I Wake Up Cryin'.

*Summer Holiday*                                    Jan. 1963

Seven Days To A Holiday, Summer Holiday, Let Us Take You For A Ride, Les Girls, Round And Round, Foot Tapper, Stranger In Town, Orlando's Mime, Bachelor Boy, A Swingin' Affair, Really Waltzing, All at Once, Dancing Shoes, Jugoslav Wedding, The Next Time, Big News.

*Cliff's Hit Album*                                    July 1963

Move It, Living Doll, Travellin' Light, A Voice In The Wilderness, Fall In Love With You, Please Don't Tease, Nine Times Out Of Ten, I Love You, Theme For A Dream, A Girl Like You, When The Girl In Your Arms Is The Girl In Your Heart, The Young Ones, I'm Looking Out The Window, Do You Want To Dance.

*When In Spain*                                    Sept. 1963

Perfidia, Amor Amor Amor, Frenesi, You Belong To My Heart, Vaya Con Dios, Sweet & Gentle, Maria No Mas, Kiss, Perhaps Perhaps Perhaps, Magic Is The Moonlight, Carnival, Sway.

*Wonderful Life*                                    July 1964

Wonderful Life, A Girl In Every Port, Walkin', A Little Imagination, Home, On The Beach, In The Stars, We Love A Movie, Do You Remember, What've I Gotta Do, Theme For Young Lovers, All Kinds Of People, A Matter of

Moments, Youth and Experience.

*Aladdin And His Wonderful Lamp*         *Dec. 1964*

Emperor Theme: Chinese Street Scene, Me Oh My, I Could Easily Fall (In Love With You), Little Princess, This Was My Special Day, I'm In Love With You, There's Gotta Be A Way, Ballet: (Rubies, Emeralds, Sapphires, Diamonds), Dance Of The Warriors, Friends, Dragon Dance, Genie With The Light Brown Lamp, Make Ev'ry Day A Carnival, Widow Twankey's Song, I'm Feeling Oh So Lovely, I've Said Too Many Things, Evening Comes, Havin' Fun.

*Cliff Richard*         *Apr. 1965*

Angel, Sway, I Only Came To Say Goodbye, Take Special Care, Magic Is The Moonlight, House Without Windows, Razzle Dazzle, I Don't Wanna Love You, It's Not For Me To Say, You Belong To My Heart, Again, Perfidia, Kiss, Reelin' And Rockin'.

*More Hits—By Cliff*         *July 1965*

It'll Be Me, The Next Time, Bachelor Boy, Summer Holiday, Dancing Shoes, Lucky Lips, It's All In The Game, Don't Talk To Him, I'm The Lonely One, Constantly, On The Beach, A Matter Of Moments, The Twelfth Of Never, I Could Easily Fall (in Love With You).

*When In Rome*         *Aug. 1965*

Come Prima, Volare, Autumn Concerto, The Questions, Maria's Her Name, Don't Talk To Him, Just Say I Love Her, Arriverderci Roma, Carina, A Little Grain Of Sand, House Without Windows, Che Cosa Del Farai Mio Amore, Tell Me You're Mine.

*Love Is Forever*         *Nov. 1965*

Everyone Needs Someone To Love, Long Ago & Far Away, All Of A Sudden My Heart Sings, Have I Told You Lately That I Love You, Fly Me To The Moon, A Summer Place, I Found A Rose, My Foolish Heart, Through The Eye Of A Needle, My Colouring Book, I Walk Alone, Someday (You'll Want Me To Want You), Paradise Lost, Look Homeward Angel.

*Kinda Latin*         *May 1966*

Blame It On The Bossa Nova, Blowing In The Wind, Quiet

Night Of Quiet Stars, Eso Beso, The Girl From Ipanema, One Note Samba, Fly Me To The Moon, Our Day Will Come, Quando Quando Quando, Come Closer To Me, Meditation, Concrete & Clay.

*Finders Keepers*                                        *Dec. 1966*
Finders Keepers, Time Drags By, Washerwoman, La La La Song, My Way, Oh Senorita, Spanish Music-Fiesta, This Day, Paella, Medley—(Finders Keepers, My Way, Paella, Fiesta), Run To The Door, Where Did The Summer Go, Into Each Life Some Rain Must Fall.

*Cinderella*                                             *Jan. 1967*
Welcome To Stonybroke, Why Wasn't I Born Rich, Peace and Quiet, The Flyder And The Spy, Poverty, The Hunt, In The Country, Come Sunday, Dare I Love Him Like I Do, If Our Dreams Came True, Autumn, The Kings Place, She Needs Him More Than Me, Hey Doctor Man.

*Don't Stop Me Now*                                      *Apr. 1967*
Shout, One Fine Day, I'll Be Back, Heartbeat, I Saw Her Standing There, Hang On To A Dream, You Gotta Tell Me, Homeward Bound, Good Golly Miss Molly, Don't Make Promises, Move It, Don't, Dizzy Miss Lizzy, Baby It's You, My Babe, Save The Last Dance For Me.

*Good News*                                              *Oct. 1967*
Good News, It Is No Secret, We Shall Be Changed, 23rd Psalm, Go Where I Send Thee, What a Friend We Have in Jesus, All Glory Laud and Honour, Just a Closer Walk With Thee, The King of Love My Shepherd Is, Mary What You Gonna Name That Pretty Little Baby, When I Survey the Wondrous Cross, Take My Hand Precious Lord, Get on Board Little Children, May the Good Lord Bless and Keep You.

## B. FILMS

*Serious Charge*
Starring: Anthony Quayle, Sarah Churchill and Andrew Ray. Cliff had a small part.
Director: Terrence Young.
Producer: Michael Delamar.

*Expresso Bongo*
Starring: Laurence Harvey, Yolande Donlan, Sylvia Syms.
Director and Producer: Val Guest.
Story: Wolf Mankowitz.


*The Young Ones*
Starring: Robert Morley, Carole Gray, The Shadows.
Director: Sidney J. Furie.
Producer: Kenneth Harper.
Choreographer: Herbert Ross.
Original Story and Screenplay: Peter Myers and Ronald
    Cass.
Background Score, Orchestrations and Musical Direction:
    Stanley Black.


*Summer Holiday*
Starring: Lauri Peters, The Shadows, with David Kossoff,
    Ron Moody, Melvyn Hayes, Teddy Green, Jeremy
    Bulloch, Una Stubbs, Pamela Hart, Jacqueline Daryl.
Director: Peter Yates.
Producer: Kenneth Harper.
Choreographer: Herbert Ross.
Original Story and Screenplay: Peter Myers and Ronald
    Cass.


*Wonderful Life*
Starring: Walter Slezak, Susan Hampshire, The Shadows
    and Melvyn Hayes, Una Stubbs, Richard O'Sullivan,
    Derek Bond.
Director: Sidney J. Furie.
Producer: Kenneth Harper.
Associate Producer: Andrew Mitchell.
Choreographer: Gillian Lynne.
Original Story and Screenplay: Peter Myers and Ronald
    Cass.
Background Score, Orchestrations and Musical Direction:
    Stanley Black.

*Finders Keepers*
Starring: The Shadows, Robert Morley, Peggy Mount, Graham Stark, Vivienne Ventura.
Director: Sidney Hayer.
Producer: George H. Brown.
Original Story: George H. Brown.
Choreographer: Malcomb Clare.
Screenplay: Michael Pertwee.
Music and Lyrics: The Shadows.

*Two a Penny*
Starring: Cliff Richard, Dora Bryan and Avril Angers, and introducing Ann Holloway.
Director: James F. Collier.
Producer: Frank W. Jacobson.
Screenplay: Stella Linden.
Music and Lyrics: Cliff Richard.
Background Score: Mike Leander.

## C. STAGE SHOWS

*Stars in Your Eyes* at the London Palladium, June to December 1960.
Starring: Cliff, Russ Conway, Joan Regan, Edmund Hockridge, David Kossoff and The Shadows.

*Blackpool Opera House*, six weeks beginning August 28th, 1961.

*Holiday Carnival* at The A.B.C. Theatre, Blackpool, June to September 1963.
Starring: Cliff and The Shadows with Carole Gray, Arthur Worsley, Dailey and Wayne, Norman Collier and Ugo Garrido.

*Aladdin and his Wonderful Lamp* at the London Palladium, December 1964 to April 1965.
Starring: Cliff and The Shadows, Arthur Askey, Una Stubbs, Charlie Cairoli and Company.
Music and Lyrics: The Shadows.

*Talk of the Town* London, February to March 1966. Cabaret with The Shadows.

*Cinderella* at the London Palladium, December 1966 to April 1967.

Starring: Cliff and The Shadows, Pippa Steel, Hugh Lloyd and Terry Scott.

Music and Lyrics: The Shadows.